THE WENDELL COCKTAIL

the WENDELL COCKTAIL

Depression, Addiction, and Beauty

MARGARET R. MILES

CASCADE *Books* • Eugene, Oregon

THE WENDELL COCKTAIL
Depression, Addiction, and Beauty

Copyright © 2012 Margaret R. Miles. All rights reserved. Except for brief quotations in critical publications or reviews, no part of this book may be reproduced in any manner without prior written permission from the publisher. Write: Permissions, Wipf and Stock Publishers, 199 W. 8th Ave., Suite 3, Eugene, OR 97401.

Cascade Books
An Imprint of Wipf and Stock Publishers
199 W. 8th Ave., Suite 3
Eugene, OR 97401

www.wipfandstock.com

ISBN 13: 978-1-61097-731-9

Cataloging-in-Publication data:

Miles, Margaret R. (Margaret Ruth), 1937–

    The Wendell cocktail : depression, addiction, and beauty / Margaret R. Miles.

    xiv + 96 p. ; 23 cm. —Includes bibliographical references.

    ISBN 13: 978-1-61097-731-9

    1. Miles, Wendell K., 1950–2010. 2. Depressed persons—United States—Biography. 3. Drug addiction. I. Title.

Manufactured in the U.S.A.

For Wendell K. Miles
September 7, 1950–April 22, 2010

CONTENTS

Preface · ix
Acknowledgments · xiii

Introduction · 1

PART 1 *Wendell's Journals*
- *one* Themes · 7
- *two* Family · 11
- *three* Childhood · 18
- *four* Nature and Beauty · 23
- *five* Animals · 26
- *six* Mental Illness · 30
- *seven* Philosophical Thoughts · 33
- *eight* Religion · 36

PART 2 *The Last Five Years*
- *nine* 2005 · 41
- *ten* 2006 · 44
- *eleven* 2007 · 48
- *twelve* 2008 · 59
- *thirteen* 2009 · 70

PART 3 *Margaret's Journals*
- *fourteen* The Last Few Days · 83

Epilogue 87
Bibliography 95

The rich and the happy can choose to keep silent,
no need to bid for attention.
But the desperate must reveal themselves,
must say: I am blind
or: I am going blind
or: It's not good for me here on Earth
or: My child is sick
or: I am not holding it together ...

But when is that really enough?
So, lest people pass them by like objects,
sometimes they sing.

And sometimes their songs are beautiful.

—RAINER MARIA RILKE, "THE VOICES"[1]

---

1. Macy and Barrows, *A Year with Rilke*, 316.

PREFACE

Wendell, my brother and youngest sibling, died a year ago. His memorial gathering was June 6, 2010—not a service, since Wendell had no formal religion; indeed, he was angry throughout his life about the judgmental fundamentalism of our childhood home. This is what I said about him at the memorial:

> We have gathered today to remember and be grateful for the life of our brother, partner, uncle, cousin, and friend, Wendell Miles. Wendell didn't like formal occasions, and we wanted his memorial to be an occasion that he could have enjoyed, so we chose to do a simple "gathering" in order to remember him together. What I think we do when we remember someone, is that each of us brings the part of the person that we have known to share with others who knew other parts of him. We put the pieces of our experience of him together in order to recreate the person we have known, to re-member him.
>
> I was thirteen years old when Wendell was born. Our mother was forty-three and she tired easily, so I did a lot of babysitting. I can't remember if it was every day or only several days a week that Mother handed him to me when I came home from school. I was to keep wheeling him around in the stroller until dinnertime. Often I took him across the Fremont Bridge in Seattle to the public library. He was usually content to sit quietly for an hour or so, eating Cheerios and looking at picture books while I enjoyed reading books that Mother had not censored. But one day he was especially fussy, and when I brought him home for dinner I told Mother that when we were crossing the bridge I felt like throwing him in Lake Union. Her reaction to that unfortunate bit of honesty was to forbid me to take him to the library anymore!
>
> Wendell told me that the smell of tar always made him feel happy. He associated the smell with a day when he was six or

Preface

seven. Walking home from school he felt excited and happy because that afternoon he was going to the birthday party of a boy he liked. Workmen were paving the road, and the smell of tar was very strong, bonding for life in his psyche with his happy feeling that day.

One of my happiest times with Wendell was a month-long vacation my husband and I spent with him on the Greek island of Syphnos in 1987. We sunned, ate, and drank; in the evening we sat outside and watched the owners of the little house we rented changing the irrigation channels in the surrounding fields. Owen and Wendell rented motorbikes and traveled all over the island. I was too scared, but I was very content to spend an afternoon alone on the beach with a good book. As they prepared to set forth, it amused me greatly to see flies lining up on their shoulders for a free ride to the next village.

From a very early age Wendell suffered from depression, which often caused him to withdraw from the company of even—or especially—those dearest to him. In his last years he was fortunate to find a loving companion who understood his need for solitude, yet was ready to be with him when his loneliness became more painful than his need to be alone.

Wendell was a passionate and energetic seeker throughout his life. He did not find a religious orientation that entirely suited him, but he loved, and to love is to participate in the great life-giving universal love. He loved beauty of all kinds, especially nature, animals, and growing plants, both flowers and vegetables. He lived quietly, enjoying his garden and hiking with his dog Maggie in the beautiful landscapes surrounding his home in Colville, Washington. He loved music and he loved to read; he tackled and understood some difficult philosophical books, mostly urged on him by me. He also spent a great deal of time writing. Writing was his psychotherapy and his way of wrestling with the difficult philosophical and religious questions that plagued him throughout his adult life. Notebook after notebook is filled with his musings—and his rants.

Wendell found institutional environments especially difficult to tolerate. I happened to call him on the day in March 2010 after he checked himself out of the hospital "against medical advice." He described to me the euphoria he had experienced that evening simply sitting at home in his favorite chair. Maybe it was not wise to leave the hospital, although by then it was probably already too late. And it was certainly worth it to him for those hours of bliss in his own home.

Preface

Wendell's memorial was held in a hunters' lodge that was just the right amount of funky for Wendell. His companion, Rita, decorated it with flowers and pictures of Wendell. Usually, memorials are for the comfort of the survivors, but in this situation there was considerable confusion as to how that might be achieved since the people who loved him were of different religious persuasions. So Rita and I decided that we would try our best to do everything as Wendell would have wanted. And I think we did.

About thirty people came. People spoke about their experiences with Wendell. There was a slide show—pictures of Wendell and pictures taken by Wendell, who was quite a good amateur photographer. Maggie, Wendell's beloved golden retriever, was there. She was perfectly behaved, greeting everyone, not barking or otherwise intrusive.

Dennis, Wendell's brother-in-law, told a story about a camping trip with Wendell shortly after Wendell's stay at the Ryther Child Center in Seattle, a treatment center for emotionally disturbed children where Wendell stayed for several months when he was eleven or twelve. They were camping in a tent in a remote area; Dennis was telling Wendell horror stories about bears. Dennis left the tent for some reason, and Wendell began to hear huge crashing noises close to the tent. He assumed it was a bear and that he would shortly be fresh meat. When Dennis returned, Wendell was cowering in a corner in fetal position. Dennis laughed and told him that he had made the noise in order to scare him. Everyone at the memorial gathering laughed, but there seemed to me to be nothing remotely funny about scaring to the point of abject terror a boy who was already suffering from emotional disturbance.

I too told of an incident I thought of as humorous, but Wendell found painful. Later, reading his journal, I found that he interpreted my passing wish that I could be relieved of caring for him (by throwing him over the bridge into Lake Union) as revealing deep resentment of him. It is indeed ironic that these two stories were told—but not from his perspective—at his memorial gathering.

The next morning Rita and I drove to a private park where Wendell had often hiked. We hiked in for fifteen minutes and came to a bridge over rushing water. Rita had brought flowers, sage, and the sunflowers Wendell loved to grow, as well as some little flowers that grow spontaneously all over his property. We threw them into the stream along with Wendell's ashes, watching as they all rushed away in the churning brook that flows into a river that flows into the ocean. My belief is that Wendell's life is not dead;

Preface

life cannot die, but only leaves the exhausted body and rushes out to other forms. We all come from, and return to, the great circulation of life in the universe. Life, in the profoundest sense, goes on.

This book does not exist to assuage my sorrow or even to commemorate Wendell's life. Wendell's condition is, in fact, an immense and accelerating social problem. Richard J. McNally, professor of psychology at Harvard University, writes, "Nearly 50 percent of Americans have been mentally ill at some point in their lives, and more than a quarter have suffered from mental illness in the past twelve months. Madness, it seems, is rampant in America."[2] Moreover, approximately half of the mentally ill also suffer from an addiction. Yet no effective treatment has been found for people with coexisting conditions. Realistic mental health professionals are resigned to acknowledging that the goal of finding a "cure" is much too dramatic and is ultimately self-defeating; harm reduction is possible, however, along with recognition that cure "is never up to us . . . it's within them or not."[3]

> The issue in medical practice is always how best to help a patient. If a cure is possible and probable without doing greater harm, then cure is the objective. . . . In many cases it's futile to dream of a cure. . . . Harm reduction means making the lives of afflicted human beings more bearable, more worth living.[4]

---

2. McNally, *What Is Mental Illness?*, 1.
3. Maté, *Hungry Ghosts*, 12.
4. Ibid., 332.

ACKNOWLEDGMENTS

AROUND THE TIME OF Wendell's illness and death several friends listened, beyond the call of duty, to my pain and bewilderment. I am especially grateful to my husband, Owen C. Thomas, my daughter, Susan Burris Haslerig, and my friends Leslie Ewing and Jane Gillette. A psychotherapist friend, Patricia Spurling Lindstrom, read the manuscript, made valuable suggestions, and companioned me as I thought through the issues.

INTRODUCTION

THIS IS WENDELL'S STORY, but like every story, his occurred in a context. The men in my family of origin, over the several generations I have known at first hand, have suffered from increments of debilitating depression. Grandfather Brown was mildly depressed. Some days he would disappear into his study and remain there all day, resuming ordinary family relations the next day. My father, Kenneth, had worse depression; he attempted to deal with it by establishing two careers and moving back and forth between them. He was a Baptist minister until church squabbles drove him to acquire an MA degree so that he could teach—a career he loved, but the inevitable frustrations of which also, several times, drove him back to ministry. He retired in his mid-fifties, unable to bear the social interactions of either workplace.

Wendell struggled against depression from childhood and throughout his too short life. He married as a young adult, and for several years he owned and managed a house painting business, earning money that, wisely invested, gave him the freedom to make a living for the rest of his life by cautiously moving his stocks around. He was also able to buy property, which afforded him the garden he loved and a small second house from which he drew a modest rental income. But he learned gradually that he could neither work among people nor live with anyone. His journals describe his life and thoughts from youth to shortly before his death, five months before his sixtieth birthday.

The world according to Wendell was a bleak place, interrupted now and then by beauty or humor. I do not doubt that his journals describe accurately his experience, but they also reflect with precision his mental illness, his obsessive fixation on real or imagined abuse, persecution, and "belittling." Wendell ignored positive experience in the interest of demonstrating mistreatment. No doubt a person without his mental disabilities would have worked with a lighter and more colorful palette of experience.

The Wendell Cocktail

I do not seek to minimize the harshness of his life as he experienced and interpreted it, but he *was* loved, however awkwardly or misguidedly by his parents, sisters, and friends. To take his mental illness seriously is to recognize that his perspective was held in its implacable grip.

My son, Ric, has suffered from depression from teenage years to the present (he is now in his fifties). He medicates with alcohol and street drugs. He has not been able to sustain any employment and lives alone in a trailer that his father and I purchased for him several years ago. Depression and alcohol organize his life. His coexisting conditions—mental illness and addiction—are *only beginning to be recognized and addressed by mental health professionals.* Until now, twelve-step programs, which address addictions of all sorts, largely ignore mental illness, and those who treat mental illness—primarily psychiatrists and psychologists—often do not accept addicts as patients.

A friend reminds me that twelve-step programs can help people with mental illness as well as addiction. The program offers a blueprint for living to anyone who commits to working the twelve steps. The problem is that mental illness often prevents a person from recognizing that the program could *help* toward a better life. Also, withdrawal from addiction is stressful, and mentally ill people frequently need prescription drugs to alleviate their anxiety. Since AA meetings have agenda expedited by members, there is no professional who can write prescriptions. So approximately half of all people with mental illness medicate with an addiction. As my son put it in a 1992 letter to me, "There's no way I'm going to give up alcohol; it *helps*, allowing me to escape momentarily; it gives me a short period of peace of mind." No one who has not experienced the desperation of mental illness can understand the pain that drives every addict to whatever *helps*.[1] As Wendell wrote in his journal:

> *7/25/03*
>
> *Intoxication has huge drawbacks, but so does sobriety. So where does that put me? In order to try to abstain, you at least have to see something to hang onto, a handle, a rope; otherwise sobriety becomes an unlivable state.*

Wendell promised himself that he would try everything that contemporary society had to offer for alleviating his mental pain before resorting

---

1. Freud wrote: "We cannot do without palliative remedies. . . . Something of this kind is indispensable." *Civilization and Its Discontents*, 75.

to suicide. He went to psychoanalysts and psychotherapists, so annoying several of them by his refusal to entertain their suggestions that they terminated his therapy. He tried drugs of all sorts—prescription and street drugs. Those who knew him best say that he drank heavily.[2] I do not know if he tried twelve-step groups, but I do know that he would have been anything but the ideal participant. When worst came to worst, he told me, he got by on "guts and dignity."

He had not had shock therapy, so he had not tried everything, but at least once he reneged on his promise to himself. Rita, his companion of fourteen years, told me that on one occasion he swallowed many pills, called to tell her, and pled with her not to call 911. She kept him awake, walking around and vomiting, for a weekend. Then she told him that if he ever did that again she would immediately call 911; she would not, could not, go through that again. He kept a gun for many years in case, he told her, the suffering became too great to endure.[3]

I don't know if I'm sadder about his life or his death. He suffered in mind and body for almost all his life: in mind, from paralyzing depression; in body, from two accidents. In his late teens, he fell from a tree and hurt his back, which gave him pain for the rest of his life; in his early twenties, he dove into the Tuolumne River, hitting a rock and permanently injuring his neck. He also suffered from Tourette's syndrome for most of his life, jerking his head and clearing his throat every few seconds or minutes. Even in a medical coma, dying, jerking gripped his frail body.

His death could be regarded either as medical neglect or as the result of suicidal behavior. He died of endocarditis, an infection of the lining of the heart that is usually treatable, in early stages, with a simple antibiotic. His doctor, determined to find cancer, prescribed test after test while Wendell's endocarditis remained untreated. He waited a month for a colonoscopy appointment while there was blood in his urine; he was coughing blood, and he had petechiae (blood spots indicating infection) all over his body. Then he had a series of strokes; by the time he received adequate medical attention, all his organs were damaged irreparably. Since he was unmarried and had no children, I, his eldest sibling, was responsible for taking him off life support.

---

2. Fingarette, *Heavy Drinking*, 59.

3. Approximately 10 to 15 percent of people with depression eventually kill themselves.

PART 1

Wendell's Journals

one

THEMES

In 2007 Wendell wrote to me:

> Margi, I have a request: that you read my writings and release them as you see fit. I have written over five hundred handwritten pages of my thoughts, and I can't think of anyone I'd rather trust to care for them. I want no editing, just spelling corrections as my mind is always ahead of my thoughts. At some point I will send these writings to you.

Wendell wanted others to read his journals. In the absence of a spouse or children who might later defend his memory, his journals were his defense against the "belittling" he experienced both as a child and an adult.

> Some people call my writing obsessive, but I think it's the most natural thing to do, especially when you consider that I have no children to say, yes, he thought this or that. It is important to me that someone know my thoughts after I am ashes. This may or may not occur, but in the hope that it will, I carry on.

Despite his denial that he had any self-esteem, the fact that he kept journals indicates that on some level he thought that his life had value and was worthy of recording.

> I must be flawed to even put together something like this journal. I sit here and write about myself and some would see that as narcissistic, but it's all I know. Has it helped me? I'm not sure. It reveals that I am more than one person; I have several strong different personalities. I write to try to understand what I've been through.

The Wendell Cocktail

I was unable to read Wendell's journals when he offered them. I had several projects underway at the time, and his journals were in difficult-to-read handwriting with multiple spelling errors. He wrote in lined workbooks, the pages splashed with various liquids and reeking of smoke. Clearly, reading them would take a great deal of time. Moreover, some of them seemed to be written while he was drunk and/or stoned; words and phrases were frequently omitted, so that sometimes I had to guess at his meaning. I told him that I would read them when I could, but when he died three years later, I still had not read them. I read them two months after his death, in deep grief and, yes, some guilt that I had not managed to read them while he was alive. Persistently, the old temptation to think that I could have done something to "save" him gripped me. Recognizing that thought as temptation to despair, however, does not cancel the fact that I could have been more attentive to his mental and physical suffering. After his death I read his journals—weeping, talking back to him, and transcribing seventy-five single-spaced pages of his thoughts.

I considered simply offering Wendell's journals as he specified, unedited and uncorrected (except spelling). But in that case, readers would have been catapulted, without warning, into the mind of an illness—frightening, even terrifying—and without the loving voice of the person he chose "to care for" his journals. So I have edited and deleted, as well as corrected spelling, in order to notice and comment, not only on Wendell's anguish, but also on the broad range of his sensibilities and interests, the wealth of his life.

As I read I realized that he wanted me finally to understand how much—how continuously and severely—he suffered. But suffering is ultimately unremarkable; as a 1960s song lyric says, "I know you've suffered much but in this you are not so alone." I decided to "release" them, or parts of them, not primarily to demonstrate his suffering, though that will inevitably be evident, but to explore the complexity of his mental illness—the particular combination of profundity, beauty, anger, and bitterness the journals reveal.

Part 1 of this book is organized by themes that recur in Wendell's journals before 2005. Part 2, which consists of journal entries from 2005 until his death in 2010, is organized by year, making evident the cumulative concentration and urgency of the thoughts of his last years. I occasionally include quotations from philosophers with whom Wendell shared amazingly similar worldviews, though he had not read them. Transcribing Wendell's journals, thinking with him and alongside him, talking back to him: this was my way of grieving Wendell's death, which felt to me so premature. His death wounded and enervated me, and for a writer, as Saul Bellow observed, "The only sure cure is to write a book."[1]

Some initial observations: Wendell often referred to himself in the third person, sometimes switching back and forth from first person to third person in the same paragraph. He also used second person (*you*) when referring to himself. Infrequently, he addressed an imagined reader directly. For example:

> *If you've gotten this far, you deserve a break, a short announcement of my great childhood love, Penny Von Pine. We were both eight years old. On Valentine's Day we both made a ring out of red paper and gave it to each other. We knew we would be together forever. I brought her home to meet my mom. As they talked I saw a long string of mucous flowing down her upper lip, slipping back and forth as she tried very casually to nip the flow from whence it came. Our love was over, at least mine was; a total of three days made up our life together.*

Most of the journal entries are undated; when there is a date, I include it. If an entry is dated, I have assumed that the whole notebook was written close to that time. In deference to readers' toleration, I omit a great deal of Wendell's repetitive rants against individuals, primarily his family, whom he felt—probably accurately—did not understand him. I have retained some repetition because Wendell obsessed on certain topics, often returning to earlier descriptions of his childhood suffering and adding detail.

Wendell articulated a worldview and perspective that most people refuse to see, a vision that has been repeatedly described by philosophers, mystics, and artists such as Dostoevsky, Kafka, Blake, Rouault, Kierkegaard, Thoreau, Pascal, Nietzsche, Freud, Becker, and numerous others. This subversive vision—subversive to superficial social cheerfulness—is not simply a view of the so-called dark side; it is also a richer and, let us acknowledge, more accurate account of the full spectrum of human experience than most people can tolerate. We who consider ourselves "normal" sacrifice some of the inassimilable, indigestible richness of human life in order to adopt the interruptible lives required by our culture of technology—email, cell phones, media entertainment—and our acquisitive enterprises.

---

1. Wieseltier, "Saul Bellow's Quest for the Vernacular Sublime," 13.

The Wendell Cocktail

Wendell's journals reveal the difficulty and imprecision of contemporary diagnoses and prescriptions for "mental illness." In fact, the phrase itself invites us to dismiss those who experience the world, its pain and its beauty, with far greater sensitivity than do most of us who pride ourselves on dealing well with social interactions. In fact, the mental illness from which my grandfather, father, and brother suffered, and which now afflicts my son (and many others), renders diagnosis virtually impossible. And accurate diagnoses are essential for identifying effective therapeutic responses. For example, for Wendell there was a bipolar aspect in his presenting unipolar depression; his journals describe not only anguish and anger but also an acute sense of beauty, of taking rich pleasure in his garden, his dog, and the rural landscapes in which he loved to hike. Across the years, from his childhood to his death, doctors have diagnosed him as having OCD (obsessive-compulsive disorder), ADHD (attention deficit/hyperactivity disorder), borderline personality disorder, and schizophrenia. He also had Tourette's syndrome.[2] Because of Wendell's complex and contradictory mental illnesses, I call him "the Wendell cocktail."

In short, the intergenerational picture, from my grandfather to my son, is one of increments of mental illness. Whether the cause is genetic, or whether the illness is mysteriously "passed on" from generation to generation in family assumptions, interactions, and worldviews, doesn't really matter.[3] Although psychopathologists agree that "genes heighten risk for mental disorder," they do not foreordain disease.[4] Let's start with family.

---

2. Patients "often meet criteria for more than one diagnosis.... We target discrete symptoms with treatments, and other drugs are piled on top to treat side effects." Angell, "The Epidemic of Mental Illness: Why?," 20–22; quoting Daniel Carlat, *Unhinged: The Trouble with Psychiatry: A Doctor's Revelations about a Profession in Crisis*. "Guided purely by symptoms," Carlat writes, "we try different drugs, with no real conception of what we are trying to fix, or of how the drugs are working. I am perpetually astonished that we are effective for so many patients."

3. "[M]ental disorders run in families.... The risk for schizophrenia [for example] is about ten times higher among the siblings and offspring of people with the disorder than it is among the general population." McNally, *What Is Mental Illness?*, 159.

4. Ibid., 160.

two

FAMILY

A CENTRAL THEME OF Wendell's journals, and of family attempts to understand him, is a fundamental and nonnegotiable clash of perspectives. To our parents—to all of us at one time or another—his behavior seemed selfish, self-centered, prideful, irresponsible, classic Lutheran *incurvatus in se*. But from another perspective, *his* perspective, he was helpless, a person suffering from a disease as dramatic and implacable as cancer, as he repeatedly said.

> *Dad had no sympathy or consideration for depression. He thought of it as a spiritual problem till the day he died. Yet he regarded physical ailments as valid and real. People like these are living in the dark ages and there are many of them.*

Wendell described himself as basically gentle and kind, a lover of beauty and silence. He acknowledged that he had a great deal of anger; when annoyed, he confessed, he would "lash out" blindly—a result, he said, of his illness. What were the family dynamics that contributed to his illness? I'm afraid it's a long story with an infinitely receding origin.

Dad's father was a farmer in eastern Ontario. He became wealthy; as he put it, "the Lord blessed him" for his principled growing of strawberries in rich soil in which everyone else grew tobacco. Most of his money went to "the missionaries" when he died. Dad's relatives were rural people with simple wants, generous spirits, and ungrammatical English. Dad left the farm for the city and education. Language and speech fascinated him; he became a speech teacher and a preacher. Priding himself on his flawless English, he read the dictionary in search of interesting words. Over his desk hung a plaque that read, "Thy speech maketh thee known" (Matt 26:73).

The Wendell Cocktail

He had a fine and subtle ear for regional accents. As he emerged from anesthesia after heart surgery, he told us the exact region in Australia from which his surgeon came. He deplored the moderating effect of television newscasters on American accents. *Not at the time*, but subsequently, I have been grateful for his constant correction of his children's speech.

Our father was a fundamentalist Baptist minister. His beliefs were founded on his passionate love for God and Scripture, most evident when he preached. With his well-worn and underlined Bible in hand, he clearly relished the exploration and interpretation of "God's word." His delight was palpable and communicable. Confidence that he accurately apprehended God's character and commands authorized him to pursue his mission with persistence and fervor. To neglect to point sinners to God at every opportunity would, in his view, have been the most reprehensible cowardice and laziness. Repeatedly throughout his life, people complained of his aggressive "witnessing." Once, while he was on a rare vacation in Hawaii, a young man remarked to him in a friendly way, "Hot as hell today, isn't it!" Father replied, "Young man, I hope you never find out how hot hell is!" A woman in a convalescent home where he played his violin and preached actually hit him, saying, "Go home and play your violin!" But "persecution" was nothing more than evidence that he was "doing the Lord's work."

However, his most painful persecution occurred to him through the problems suffered by his children. The physical and emotional troubles caused, or exacerbated, by the pressures of a fundamentalist worldview and childrearing methods, might have prompted a less confident man to examine his own part in creating these problems. To Dad they demonstrated simply that one who does "the Lord's work" may expect the devil to use every possible means to undermine, harm, and attempt to destroy him.

Mary, our mother, was the daughter of intrepid parents—immigrants from England to what they considered the "wilds" of Canada. She was beautiful, pious, and neurasthenic; as a young woman, she dropped out of nurse's training because of "nerves." After denying herself what she described as a "purely sexual attraction" to another man, she met our father. Her attraction to him was "intellectual" and thus acceptable. Days of awkward silence followed her timid request to her father to marry this young, fervent minister who came from a farm. They married on August 21, 1936.

Wendell was born when our mother was forty-three. He was unplanned and unexpected, with three older sisters. Mother, like most people in 1950, thought that a woman over forty was too old for childbearing.

Family

After his birth, she definitely did not want to take the chance that she would become pregnant again. Whether consciously planned to avoid that possibility or not, she set Wendell up in a twin bed in her room. My father slept in the basement, strongly resenting Wendell for effectively blocking his access to sexual intercourse. Mother used Wendell to save her from sex, which, she once told me, was "the cross I've always had to bear."

Father took his anger and frustration out on Wendell, a little boy. In the circumstance, neither Mother nor Father behaved like adults. But let me try to imagine them more richly. Both parents were helpless, completely unskilled in addressing problems directly. They had never seen their parents discuss disagreements or difficulties. They were afraid to acknowledge their discomfort with each other because within their religious worldview, divorce was not a possibility. Moreover, they were immigrants in a country they considered hostile, a country whose values they judgmentally characterized as "Hollywood." They had rigid and nonnegotiable standards that they believed God himself laid on them. I weep for them, but oh, the harm they did! This was the emotional-environmental part of Wendell's mental illness. He didn't usually blame his mother for her part in creating an unsustainable home environment.

Wendell was convinced that his mental illness was genetic, but he also insisted that a more loving and supportive childhood would have made a great difference in his life.[1] In the following entry, Wendell cites genetic flaws as causing his illness, but then immediately invokes the environment of his childhood home.

> *How can one fight against such a monstrous enemy as heredity, genes? No matter how I try I am overwhelmed by my parents' joylessness. Dad has written about his own realization that he wasn't a good father, but he denies that he was a bad father. But he was a bad father, and until his last year the only quasi-apology he said to me was that "sometimes I feel that I haven't given you anything." At the time I didn't know how to respond other than to comfort him by saying, "Oh no, you've given me a lot of garden tools." Later, however,*

---

1. McNally, *What Is Mental Illness?*, 181–82. McNally suggests that a method of analyzing "Gene X Environment" is needed. "A gene is expressed only when its DNA is transcribed into RNA and translated into protein. Otherwise it remains inactive. . . . Socio-environmental factors activate processes in the central nervous system that influence the activity of hormones and neurotransmitters throughout the periphery of the body, resulting in the interaction of signaling molecules with receptors on cells that activate transcription factors. Via these pathways the environment regulates the expression of genes, either turning them on or turning them off."

The Wendell Cocktail

> *I realized that he was speaking metaphorically. Had I recognized this at the time, I think I would have said, "Do you really want to discuss this?" But at the time I did not want to hurt him. I was the kid; why did I always feel that I had to protect him? I don't know if he loved or hated me, but his actions made me feel like a rotten little boy, even when I was a man. He never said he loved me, even though I was very loving to him when I visited. When he had a heart attack I was at the hospital every day. Why could he not respond when I told him that I loved him as he was going into the operating room? He just looked down.*

People know what they do; they frequently know why they do what they do; but what they don't know is what what they do does.[2]

Did Dad intend to harm Wendell? No, but he didn't know that what he did, did. Mental illness left both Dad and Wendell with little leisure for pondering others' perspectives. Reading Wendell's journals, I frequently experienced the need to protest the suffocating constriction of his viewpoint. I wanted to say, yes, but there were other suffering people there too; I wanted to offer, not just all-around compassion, but more spacious understanding. I needed to consider what Wendell's family had to work with. I wanted to present a picture in which there were no bad guys in sight, just wall-to-wall suffering people—unprepared, unskilled, frightened people, *people who had never been in the situation before.* People who didn't have enough of anything—security, love, knowledge, money, confidence. And nobody to say, "Look, look at what you're doing. You don't mean to be doing this, but this, in fact, is what you're doing."

Mental illness affects all family members, causing emotional (and often financial) suffering to everyone who loves the ill person. The cost in suffering to my family members is, and has been, enormous. Wendell's family and friends attempted to help, offering him everything from listening to sharing our homes for periods of time. One sister actually took him on her honeymoon and offered her home to him repeatedly; he lived with another sister's family for a summer, and later, several times, for a month. His journals show that he recognized and appreciated these efforts on the part of family members, but finally bitterness trumped gratitude. In the grip of a severe depressive episode, he threatened to kill another sister for

---

2. Dreyfus and Rabinow, *Michel Foucault*, 187.

her prescription drugs when she declined to share them further. Nothing a family member or friend can do is ever enough, for the need is infinite.

Professional misunderstanding and mislabeling of family efforts on behalf of the mentally ill person frequently cause additional suffering. The National Association for Mental Illness (NAMI) lists several common clinical misinterpretations of family responses: dazed family members are frequently misinterpreted as "distant, disinterested"; "worried sick family" are misinterpreted as "over-involved, 'enmeshed'"; and angry family members can be accused of being "emotionally erratic, demanding."[3] The extent of family members' bewilderment, anxiety, and sorrow is seldom acknowledged by either friends or mental health professionals.

> *I prefer not to include you in my life. It's mine, all mine, and I am trying very hard not to let your actions consume me. The only way I know how is to be alone, apart from you.*

Wendell thought of himself as a hermit, a choice little understood within his family. He did not answer his phone until caller identification had been established—and usually not then. He could not tolerate people, perhaps especially family, coming to his home unannounced. Once, his brother-in-law appeared unexpectedly at his door in the middle of the afternoon. Wendell yelled at him, insisting that he leave his property immediately.

> A recent study has helped me understand the importance of solitude, even isolation, to (some) mentally ill patients. In her article "The 'Other' of Culture in Psychosis: The Ex-Centricity of the Subject," Ellen Corin focuses on the *experience* of mental illness, "the truth of the subject," her patients describe.[4] She argues that focusing exclusively on the biological or social aspects of mental illness does not adequately attend to its experiential dimension. Narratives suggest that something rises from within the patient's experience and destabilizes it, shaking the lived world at its roots. Patients speak of a loss of vital energy that extends to the core of their being and attacks psychological functions; they say that this initial experience invades their entire lives, blocks their capacity to express emotions or relate to people, and leads progressively to

---

3. NAMI Provider Education Program, Class 1, "Using the Medical Family Therapy and Family Consultation Models of Care in Serious Brain Disorders," 1.17.
4. Corin, "The 'Other' of Culture in Psychosis," 276.

isolation; it is a kind of 'staggering' that undermines their ability to act and to relate to the world.[5]

Studying patients in Canada and India, Corin and her colleagues sought to identify cross-cultural factors differentiating patients who required repeated rehospitalization from those who managed to avoid rehospitalization. Extensive interviews produced surprising findings. Initially, the researchers hypothesized that patients' "ability to maintain, restore, or create significant social links and to resume a valued place within society" would allow them to avoid rehospitalization, but something close to the opposite was revealed. Two primary findings appeared.

> First, the "objective" situation of the two groups of patients (frequently hospitalized and non-rehospitalized) did not greatly differ, with both groups having a paucity of interpersonal relationships with family members and the social network and an overall marginality in the area of normative social roles. Second, hospitalized patients often perceived their marginality negatively—as being imposed on them by others. . . . In contrast, the non re-hospitalized patients tended to accept or even view positively this sense of being outside. . . . [T]he sort of recovery that allowed patients to remain out of hospital required them to distance themselves from the social world.[6]

Corin and her colleagues found that "the ability to construct a personal protected space at the margins of the ordinary 'normal' world was of central importance" to patients who were not rehospitalized. They named the distance created by non-rehospitalized patients "positive withdrawal." Positive withdrawal permitted patients to create and defend an "inner space," a kind of "psychic skin" within which they could "rest and progress at their own pace."[7]

Like Corin's non-rehospitalized schizophrenic patients, Wendell avoided rehospitalization by becoming a hermit. Nothing pained him more than the imposition of social relations, whether family occasions or institutions. At the end of his life, suffering from terminal physical illness, he nevertheless checked himself out of the hospital, signing a statement acknowledging that he did so "against medical advice." His relief in being in his own home was euphoric. Similarly, Corin's patients found relief in

---

5. Ibid., 273.
6. Ibid., 280.
7. Ibid., 283.

"positive withdrawal," in solitude, rest, and quietness—the conditions necessary for protecting the porous boundaries of the fragile ego. Wendell's experience, as well as that of Corin's patients, contradicts the dominant cultural wisdom that prescribes regular participation in family and twelve-step programs for the relief and support of dual diagnosis (mental illness and addiction) patients.[8]

Yet, for many or most mentally ill people, as for healthy people, the companionship, support, and encouragement of others is crucial. *Understanding* a mentally ill person's experienced need for solitude does not necessarily coincide with agreeing that separation from family, friends, and a caring community is most beneficial. However, when a person is financially and practically able to maintain herself in solitude, family members have few grounds for insisting on either some form of group therapy or ongoing family interaction. This was Wendell's situation. His ability to maintain his chosen lifestyle allowed him to protect his isolation intransigently. When his aloneness became loneliness, he would reach out, tentatively and briefly, to a sister or a friend.

---

8. For example, NAMI lists among the goals of therapy: "to help family members join together to cope with an illness and to do so within the context of allowing the patient maximal feasible autonomy and agency." NAMI Provider Education Program 1.25.

three

CHILDHOOD

WENDELL'S SENSE OF EXTREME isolation began in childhood and continued throughout his life. His obsession with his childhood experiences was also lifelong.

> *At the age of seven I was caught smoking. My father kicked me in the side with his big shoes, and with a scowling grimace to boot! It wasn't the physical pain; I could have taken much more of that. No, it was the grimace that killed me, one I would learn very well throughout my years with my father. What did I ever do to make him angry except be born because of his lust? I was a nice-looking, even good-looking kid with a gentle personality. But when you get treated like shit, you tend to give back as you were treated.*
>
> *I remember well the onset of my illness in 1960–61. At first it was depression I kept to myself. I felt as though I'd been hit by a car or had fallen from my bike. I felt extreme anxiety and fear all the time. It was so hard to connect with people when I felt this way and "they" didn't seem to . . .*[1]
>
> *When I really broke down, not leaving the house, fearful of everything, I was suffering from severe depression with psychotic elements. I think that my symptoms would now be labeled obsessive-compulsive disorder (OCD). I was eleven years old, and my suffering seemed to be unnoticed. I yearned to be dead. This experience can never be understood by anyone who has not had it.*
>
> *When my mental illness became troublesome, my father left me with another minister's family, hoping they would heal me. He thought that the help of "the Lord's people" far surpassed any help I could get from psychiatry. But I was abused by the minister's son, who played with my penis and generally disrespected me.*

1. The text of this entry breaks off here.

In the eighth grade I had a brief reprise of my illness. I started to grow my hair in the style of the day. Dad hit me and said, "You're going to get a haircut." My hair wasn't even over my ears, but adults back then had a huge problem with hair.

My childhood family never had any fun. From the time I was eleven Dad never took us out to dinner. Before then he occasionally took us to a small cafe in Ballard where we could order only the cheapest plates. When I think about this it startles me. Why was there no fun, no joy, no happiness in our family? Isn't Christianity supposed to be the answer to unhappiness, light versus darkness? Joy versus sadness, anxiety and neglect? Why? Why? WHY? All of us, my sisters and myself, suffer deeply from this. We try to defeat the embedded pain with repression, drugs, or religion.

As a teenager I was dull, depressed, ignorant, and sad. Throughout those years I had a mixture of illness and normalcy. I still had some hope, but my sickness was always lurking. I had a temporary reprieve when I was twenty to twenty-six; I was able to forget about the terror that had been in my head from age seven to eighteen.

5/4/05

My first memory of experiencing OCD (obsessive compulsive disorder) was in 1964 when I lived with my sister and brother-in-law, Dennis and Dorothy. It was prompted by the "sounds of silence," which, in fact, were not silent. I found in the serene woods of Lake Dawn, five miles up from Port Angeles, that I could hear the blood circulating in my head. I was on Melleril at the time. In 1964 there were no other drugs than Melleril for anxiety psychosis. I was on a dose of 100 mgs twice daily, not a small dose.[2]

It frightened me to think that I could not escape, even in silence. My anxiety went on for several months although it didn't completely incapacitate me because I was an eighth grader enjoying for the first time the kids around me. I seem to have made a mark with the boys because of my next-to-largest penis. The top rating went to Junior Cipreano, a tough kid who had a full beard when he was thirteen years old.

---

2. Documenting the "astonishing increase in the numbers of the mentally ill in the United States in the last forty years," Robert Whitaker charges pharmaceutical and psychiatric organizations of concealing the dangers of long-term exposure to "psychiatric medications in increasingly complex 'cocktails.'" He alleges that these powerful medications can actually cause shrinkage of frontal lobes and loss of cognitive capacity; *Anatomy of an Epidemic*.

The Wendell Cocktail

> *I was twenty years old when I first realized that no one could rescue me. I still had hope during the Ryther years that someone could, but I was only twelve at the time.*

Wendell's resentment of his family's failure effectively to help him focused on his father. His insistence that his sisters knew nothing about family interactions when they were no longer in the home precludes my objection to the harshness with which he described our father. Honestly, I only partially recognize the father he describes, but I acknowledge that the home may have deteriorated dramatically in the years after my marriage (when Wendell was five years old). I visited the home only occasionally and briefly after my marriage. He mentions no happy times; perhaps he did not experience any, but it also seems possible, if not probable, that his illness distorted his experience.

> *Dad put everything in categories; there is only one right opinion—his. Unacknowledged issues about power and control ruled his psyche. He had learned as a young man that power and control could inhibit the side of him he feared would cause him to act in ways he abhorred. Then I came along, a reminder that the uncontrollable was still alive and well.*
>
> *He was very threatened by others with knowledge/power. He resisted science and psychology and became very confrontational with medical doctors and others with perspectives and methods different than his. After placing me in the Ryther Child Center when I was twelve years old, he disagreed with their approach and was verbally combative with the staff. I believe that my father's issues with the Ryther staff stemmed not from concern over the best treatment for me, but the fact that doctors accused him of behaving in ways that were detrimental to my health.*
>
> *Sometimes, rarely, Dad expressed his tender side. On the way to Ryther he said to me, "I'm sorry; I should never have hit you." I absorbed moments like that as a sponge does water. They were few, but I so needed to hear them. Nevertheless I always knew that I was a thorn in his side. I think I represented the outcome of his lust—after all, Mother's pregnancy was an "accident." But the primary issue was my rearing. On the one side, Mother gave me protection and love. On the other, Dad resented me. The two reactions responded to and aggravated each other.*

There is a small crayon drawing in the journal at this point, the only drawing in any of the journals. A man says, "bad boy," and a boy says, "I

Childhood

was trying to please you, helping you put seeds in the ground. I'm sorry."
The text continues:

> As I have said, my father saw me as evidence of his lust. Mother wanted no more children, and she used me to keep Dad away. So I was the dog that was kicked literally and psychologically. Later, he said that since he was fifty-five he was "too old" to hear the accusations with which my therapists said I needed to confront him. They just had no idea what a controlling dad I had. Everyone outside the family who thought as he did loved him; he was articulate and caring. For many years while my mother and I tried to get a painting business going, he was nowhere in sight. And when I would play some sweet music that my mother loved, he would emerge from the bedroom and tell us to turn it down. When I broke my neck at twenty-three and lived with Mom and Dad for the summer of 1974, Mom would come down and tell me ever so softly that I should turn the television down, even though it was already so low that at five feet I could barely hear it.
>
> By the time I entered Ryther I was damaged. The staff there helped me as much as they could, but I kept running away. They wanted to keep me for two years, but I went home after six months. But soon my parents wanted me hospitalized again, so I ran away from home like a scared animal. I was caught, but again they had to either keep me or put me somewhere else. I just grew up as best I could, a sick child.
>
> For years I lived in the stone house [in the backyard of my home]. The stone house was no more than a 6' x 10' vegetable storage hut. When I was in the tenth and eleventh grades I went there many days after school to lie on my bed in the dark and wait for the next day. However, during some of this time I worked after school and became fiercely independent. I paid for my own car insurance, and the car gave me a sense of relief and freedom. Oh yes, and there was masturbation. That was a godsend. I knelt on my army cot in the stone house and put a Playboy on the mattress and had a very fine few minutes that gave me relief. I've always appreciated this.
>
> In 1970–71, a photographer had a grant at Port Angeles, where I was living with Dennis and Dorothy, to lead a children's theater. I was a young twenty-year-old; he shot pictures of me naked standing on a rock by the ocean. I thought he truly cared, as a naïve kid would think, but what he ultimately wanted to do was to have sex with me. I learned this one night when I stayed overnight at his house on Graymarsh Farms, a beautiful 1000-acre preserve near Sequim, Washington. I don't know how many kids he abused.

The Wendell Cocktail

I'm glad that when I die I won't be anyone's father. I'll just be a brother, or cousin, or uncle of someone. They'll all forget about me in about two minutes after the memorial, if there is one. I guess I'll never know whether I was loved any more than I'll know if there is a "higher power." (How can anyone be truly honest in saying there is, or there isn't? Both seem preposterous.)

There is nothing better than to work with a friend accomplishing a perfect job, to enjoy the companionship of having a common goal, including the money that comes from a job well done. It is the best life has to offer, people working together in harmony with the goal of making something that gives the client happiness that comes from excellent work. I miss those times very much, but that wasn't enough for my friend, Mark, who had issues with alcohol which eventually brought our friendship to an end. I am so sad about this. I was then only drinking lightly, only after work, two or three beers, then anticipating the day that would follow, for which I was reasonably bright-eyed and bushy tailed. But Mark was often so hung over that he couldn't work. He tried several times to stop drinking—successfully, for four to six months at a time. When we lived together in 1994, he was an appraiser at a big bank, but this gave him no satisfaction. Every weekend he drank continually. I hoped that we could do things together, canoeing, hiking, outdoor stuff. But he preferred to be in his room drinking. Since I wasn't drinking much at that time, it was a horrible thing. Everything had changed; he had no hope left. He played music, but his music wasn't recognized, so that was his excuse to try to kill himself through carbon monoxide poisoning in his car. He finally succeeded by drinking mouthwash (which has an alcohol content of 40 percent) over a period of a year or so. Mark changed from an extremely well-liked and loved person to one who paid his rent with money his brother and I gave him. I had him at my house for five months before his death, but he was extremely intoxicated all the time. But I loved that man, as did many.

Splitting, taking off, cutting out, crashing: vernacular words for leaving. In 1981 I moved from state to state, attaching state insignias as I went. The two best months of my life were traveling around the periphery of the United States, almost always by the ocean, the Pacific, the Gulf, and the Atlantic. Then a strange voyage across Canada from Ontario to British Columbia, then down to Colville to see Dennis and Dorothy. In Saskatchewan, the temperature was in the upper 90s; I was young then, and able to handle the heat. It was before I broke my back on October 31, 1981. Canada is different, a difference I enjoyed; slower, more courteous, thoughtful, fewer rednecks, many fewer. The feeling of the 1950s. People need to travel outside the US; there's so much there.

four

NATURE AND BEAUTY

In *The Idiot*, Dostoyevsky's protagonist, Prince Myshkin, claimed that "beauty can save the world."[1] Wendell pursued beauty relentlessly—but it did not save his world. He loved music, but the natural world continued to be his primary experience of beauty. However, as Wendell saw very clearly, natural beauty is not innocent; it is also "nature red in tooth and claw." There were times when beauty terrified Wendell, even while he was tremendously attracted to seek it out.

Wendell preferred wilderness; he didn't like parks, with trees with their names posted on signs in Latin. Being uncontrolled, wild beauty can wound. Accustomed as most of us are to thinking of beauty as healing, it is difficult to understand why beauty—especially, in Wendell's case, natural beauty—can cause panic. To begin to understand, we must recognize the *power* of beauty. Power is ambiguous; it can either heal or destroy. Wendell experienced the full range of beauty's power—simultaneously. As Rainer Maria Rilke wrote, "For Beauty's nothing / but beginning of Terror we're still just able to bear . . ."[2]

> There are few moments of sparkling clarity. When they come it is a moment of peace. As long as I can remember I've sought out places of beauty and peace. Instead of experiencing beauty and peace, however, I feel melancholy. I used to sit on the pews of St. Edwards Seminary in Seattle; I went there to enjoy the church's rich beauties—high ceilings, stained glass—and I sat for hours, or walked around smelling the wonderful church. Then I walked away with great sadness, only the silence had reached me.

1. Dostoyevsky, *The Idiot*, 446.
2. Rilke, *Duino Elegies*, 21.

The Wendell Cocktail

My dreams are terrible because they are beautiful, and I can't have them in real life.

When I was seventeen years old I often walked out on the pier at Juanita Beach in Kirkland, Washington. I stared at the waters of Lake Washington, but all I felt was desolation even though natural beauty was the only solace I could find. At eleven years old I just wanted to be "put out." I wanted to be unconscious for a few days. Since this was not possible, my mind remained pained and tortured. I still wonder if I could be put into an induced coma for long enough for me to get some rest.

11/22/03

I'm looking at a red shed
someone has recently painted it
barn red
It's very old and ready to fall down
But nevertheless someone has tried to make it
look nice.
The things that "don't matter"
are often the things that very much
do matter.

Humans have only recently loved natural surroundings. As little as fifty to a hundred years ago we thought of nature as a threatening enemy. Nature was a primary cause of human suffering. But once we had formed our shelters, our protected places, we became able to appreciate the world outside. [Our attitude toward nature] has reversed to such a degree that we think of nature as our friend. But nature is careless, or at least indifferent, to walkers, hikers, and climbers. Violence created natural beauty, and violence is still a possibility when people interact with nature.

Whenever I could I lived, from two to seven days at a time, in the lakes, alpine forests, and mountains; they were my real love. I'll always feel fortunate and grateful for that experience. There are beautiful areas within twenty miles of Port Angeles, Washington, the home of my heart, such as Whiskey Bend, Elwa River Valley, Boulder Lake and Boulder Mountain. I remember them all. They will still be here for hundreds, if not thousands, maybe millions of years. I last saw Boulder Lake in 1990; I'd been there almost every year since 1979. For the adventurous there was a smaller lake one mile away by deer trail; it was a beautiful small gem with the best brown trout I'd ever eaten. Backpacking and being in the woods I felt full of strength and courage. I knew that if I had wanted to I could have stayed there for a couple of months, feeding on berries and fish.

Once, when I was hiking there with a friend, we were awakened by frightening sounds. We thought that it was a bear, and I heard Burt's heart pounding with fear. When we finally had the courage to get out of our tents we saw elk bugling under a full moon. Fear turned into a magical moment of unsurpassed awe.

When I returned alone in 1990, a lightning storm scared me. I thought I was familiar with the mountains, but I was unprepared for lightning striking so close to me. Later, as I came running down the mountain, I wasn't so afraid and I almost hoped I would be struck. There's a fine line between terror and beauty. Sometimes, in the midst of great beauty, fear of death dissolves.

I so loved being in the woods. I've hugged trees and felt more than their physical presence. It's good to know that they will still be there thousands of years from now. I would like to fly forever and ever through the Olympic Mountains, landing wherever I want, with a brain that had no past or future, just a mind that could appreciate the wonders—no fear, no anxiety, no pain. I could spend a long time in this state, a few billion years.

When backpacking you should try to leave a campsite better than you found it, a camping ethic that seems to be disappearing over the last thirty years. Boulder Lake and the Olympic Mountains have been treated rudely, people "going to the bathroom" in common trail areas, paper and other trash left on the ground. The last time I was there, 1990, I left very depressed. This had been my haven, I thought that the five-mile hike to the lake would have eliminated the disrespectful. But I was wrong. Now you have to hike ten or fifteen miles to get to uncluttered beauty—what a shame!

How can we be objective about human life? We are animals, but unlike other animals in some ways. We have nothing with which to compare human life. This puts human intelligence at a great disadvantage; we can only try to look through the eyes of history. Yet our ideas are of such small scope. I have walked though wonderful woods wondering how many of us think of the violence and time it took to carve out this beauty?

David Attenborough, a respected biologist and naturalist, said something on television last night that has long been in my mind. Something simple, something reasonable, that can't be contested or rebutted. He said, when I see all this beauty and someone says, you must believe in God, all I can say is that at the same time I am seeing and absorbing all this beauty, I can't help but think of all the children dying of starvation. When I heard this, I felt a little less alone; someone else is attuned to the suffering!

five

ANIMALS

WENDELL WAS MUCH MORE comfortable with animals than with people. He loved their companionability, empathized strongly with their vulnerability, and envied their confidence in simply being themselves. He also found them humorous.

> *I would not describe humans as looking like certain animals, for I would not like to disparage the animals.*

2/10/03

I have a king-size comforter on a queen-size bed. That was a mistake. I made a bed for Maggie, my golden retriever, at the foot of my bed. She has learned to roll on the end of the comforter to get more of it down on her bed, so that she has a back comforter as well as a floor comforter. During the night we fight for the covers. I wake up with cold shoulders, thinking I've lost the comforter until I find I can't pull it up because she's lying on it!

One day a skunk came out of the shed when I was working in the garden. It had a glass jar, like a pickle jar, stuck on its head and it came up to me and stood there. So I knelt down, grabbed his neck, and tried to pull it off. This required some force and all the while this little skunk just stood there braced. I couldn't get the jar off its head by pulling, so I took a rock and gently broke the bottle. For a few seconds the skunk looked up at me; then slowly he walked away into the bushes. That skunk somehow knew that I would help him/her, and it risked its life that I would help and not hurt it. I, of course, also risked being sprayed for my efforts. I felt honored and happy after this experience.

The chickadees start their love song in April or earlier. Those who are still at it in June have not yet met their mate. Their June song is so desperate compared to their April song. The deer, rabbits, birds and hummingbirds love my park-like property. So do the bees, yellow jackets, and mosquitoes. I have learned to live with all of these. The yellow jackets never sting or bother me, even when I turn on the water when dozens are drinking at the spout. I can put my hands in their midst and they know I won't hurt them, so they leave me alone. It's beautiful.

I was watching two finches at my bird feeder. There was no seed in the feeder, but one of the birds was pecking at nothing and kept guarding his spot, while the other tried to penetrate the first bird's space in the feeder. The first bird would peck, then look up at the other bird as if to say, look at my find and you don't get any, a total fake-out. Why? It seemed at the time that competitive natures were evident, but with no seed whatsoever?—not even remotely, as my nephew Randy would say!

I saw the remains of a California quail today in my yard, feathers left from a redtail hawk's dinner. As I was standing by the feathers I heard a new sound from its mate. I've listened carefully since they arrived but never at the end of their "a whee-who, a whee-who" have I heard a mournful "oh-oh-oh." This may be a gross misinterpretation and anthropomorphizing, but I really feel, based on my previous observations, that these little birds do have more than just survival going on in their brains.

We value pets as caregivers. Why is it that human caregivers are thought to be low on the [social] totem pole?

We have no problem putting animals down, but we humans think we're special; we have a "soul," unlike animals. I hold the contrary view; all life is special in its own way.

Yesterday there was a competition for dogs of every size and breed. A little chihuahua was in a cookie race; the first one to eat all the cookies and make it to the other side won. It was sponsored by the dog rescues/habitat and what I liked was that every dog won. But this chihuahua was having trouble getting through two-inch grass, not because it had three-inch legs, but because of his four-inch penis. He reminded me of my old friend Chumly Wadlow, a basset hound who wandered around the construction sites where I worked. He was so well endowed that he was constantly dragging his poor penis on the concrete. Some of us thought we could help him by putting a small balloon on his penis. As he walked it would slap from right to left up his backside, so many of us would laugh out loud as he came. One day we no longer saw him come by on his daily walk and we later learned that he had died. We put a small cross up for him in an adjacent empty property with the lines, Chumly: best in piece. Meaning the best hung slugger of all time.

Because of global warming, we will see species of birds in areas in which they are not normally seen.

If the Christian heaven has no animals (supposedly because they have no "soul"), I sure wouldn't want to be there. But perhaps only Christian animals would be allowed to be in attendance? The whole thing is absurd.

I've always sought passion, not necessarily sexual passion; animals have created the same passion in me. I think I could find ecstasy in the midst of lions, elephants, etc. I haven't seen the sights my grandfather saw in Africa; his painting of lions hangs above my stove. I would have liked so much to be an adult before he died in 1960. I think we had much in common, but I was only ten years old when he died. I feel cheated that I couldn't have known him as a peer. I think I would have loved him and that he could have taught me a great deal. I do know that he was a wonderful painter and that he cared deeply for animals.

The birds that flock around my birdfeeder are like little five year olds performing a ballet.

I've seen Maggie, my golden retriever, defend the property from two dogs that occasionally come up to it. She is only mildly aggressive, half concerned, half ferocious. She never makes any harsh movements, just lets them know in a very graceful way that they should leave. She's a true sweetheart.

Is what we call "soul" the ability to reflect? If this is so, many animals such as monkeys, birds, and dogs have souls.

Birds are intense, hypervigilant, always aware of their surroundings, ready to protect, looking for food. They look like little dinosaurs, which scientists now think birds evolved from. The chickadee may not survive because they are friendlier than most birds, which puts them in jeopardy because others may take advantage. Sounds like humans.

We are all animals. I've seen dogs and cats that are cleaner than some people. We shit like animals, pee like animals, and fuck like animals. Only difference is our brain happened to evolve for some reason.

Often I just want to lie in my room and listen to the birds, to every nuance of the sounds they make, nothing else. Animals have always given me the most peace; this is why I feel an obligation to feed them because I can't give them anything else. Not to see them fighting over the food, not to see the drama, but to see and hear them happy, a fantasy of communicating with them. But animals do not exist for our pleasure; they have their own life; they don't need us. Even insects have their own life, and I kill them only if it becomes a matter of me or them. I don't like to be stung, but hundreds of yellow jackets surround me and don't bother me a bit, almost as if they understood that I will not hurt them if they do not hurt me. I walk through swarms and they don't attack, only get out of the way. And in return for my not bothering them, they eat the aphids from my plants. Animals don't want to harm humans; they just want to be left alone. But they will protect their species, as we will protect ours.

Some might say, well, he couldn't get along with people so he chose animals because they couldn't talk back. But that isn't why I love them. It is their innocence, their beauty, their ability to adapt and to connect with their caregivers. Also their huge spirit—soul, if you want. They do not kill for fun, but for necessary food. Some, like cats, do play with their catch but this cannot be interpreted as malicious; even if it is, it is the exception.

six

MENTAL ILLNESS

8/26/04

Don't minimize my life, people. Thoughts, desires for knowledge, inner peace: my whole life has been in these pursuits. Some genetics are probably my worst enemy, some environmental factors. Please do not put me in a category.

THE "BIBLE" OF PSYCHIATRY, the Diagnostic and Statistical Manual of Mental Disorders, lists nine symptoms of MDD (Major Depressive Disorder): "depressed mood most of the day, nearly every day; markedly diminished interest or pleasure in nearly all activities most of the day, nearly every day (anhedonia); loss of appetite or significant weight loss or gain; insomnia or hypersomnia nearly every day; observable psychomotor agitation or retardation; fatigue nearly every day; inappropriate guilt or feelings of worthlessness; difficulty concentrating nearly every day; and recurrent thoughts of death or suicidal ideation, or suicide attempt."[1]

> *All depression is anger turned upside down, though not all who have anger suffer depression. The diagnosis given to me by the head of psychiatry at the University of Washington was "dysthymia," meaning one is always in a mild to moderate state of depression, broken only by major clinical depression at various times throughout one's life.*

Wendell exhibited all of the symptoms of MDD, but depression was a partial diagnosis. He was also bipolar: the highs were really high, and the lows were really low. Like a schizophrenic, he also needed to be alone to keep himself together; he shunned most human company most of the

---

1. McNally, *What Is Mental Illness?*, 48–49.

time.[2] In 2007 he wrote: "I often have to reconstruct myself on an hourly basis. I don't think anyone realizes just how severe this is." Was he ADD as well as OCD? Did he have PDNOS (personality disorder not otherwise specified), the third most common diagnosis?[3] What about melancholic depression, which is distinguishable, some experts argue, from MDD?[4] All of the above? To treat one diagnosis as *the* diagnosis, to "categorize" Wendell, would be hopelessly inadequate.[5]

> 9/22/04
>
> *I've been discounted a lot of my life, first because I was in Ryther Child Center, then because I had chemical dependencies. No one understands the pain except people with my mental makeup.*

Wendell was also a cutter. Although his journals do not describe his self-injury in any detail, he talked to me about it several times as an important coping tool. Self-injury is "deliberate, nonsuicidal destruction of one's own body tissue."[6]

> *I'm fifty-seven and I still bite my tongue and my lips. I make grimaces that have, though time, permanently damaged my jaws and tongue. I twist, knot, and pull my hair out . . .*

For Wendell, self-injury was "a solidly loner deviant undertaking."[7] He began this behavior well before it became a publicly known phenomenon, making me wonder if he may have thought that he was the only one who got satisfaction from self-injury, thus further consolidating his isolation. No Web sites or chat rooms existed to offer support until the practice increased, especially among teenagers, in the 1990s and early 2000s. I wonder if the many pages torn out of the journals I received describe a practice he

---

2. Some researchers argue that the distinction between schizophrenia and bipolar disorder should be abandoned. Ibid., 171.

3. Characterized by parasuicidal self-cutting, unstable self-image, "a history of stormy interpersonal relationships, and great difficulty regulating emotions, especially rage." Ibid., 185.

4. Symptoms: "profound loss of pleasure, psychomotor retardation (slowed thinking, movement and speech), agitated restlessness, appetite loss, loss of interest in sex, early morning awakening, and impaired concentration." Ibid., 189.

5. "Extensive psychiatric comorbidity undermines the expectation that diagnosis amounts to determining the one true disorder from which the patient suffers, ruling out similar conditions." Ibid., 185.

6. Adler and Adler, *Tender Cut*, 1.

7. Ibid., 107.

was ashamed of and didn't want anyone to know about. Throughout his journals Wendell described the causes and perceived benefits of self-injury.

Studies confirm Wendell's account of self-injury. The impetus can come from "feeling acutely bad," lack of grounding when emotionally overwhelmed, the need to exteriorize inner pain, self-punishment, and a need to unblock pent-up emotions. Benefits include "sensations of release from anxiety," control, and (sometimes) orgasmic euphoria. Self-injury can be an expression of anger or a desire to make one's suffering visible to others, a longing for understanding that Wendell repeatedly reports. It can also be a mode of rebellion, especially among young people.[8] In his latter years, Wendell largely replaced cutting with the use of prescription drugs and alcohol—a more socially acceptable practice, but equally or more destructive in long-term effects.

> *If I had the power my father acquired I think I would act differently. I feel that I have a warmer heart and I value tolerance and open-mindedness. But my mental problems often get in the way. If I had a clean slate and a mind without defensiveness, I could have had a very different life.*
>
> *I could have been soft and gentle, my main side.*

---

8. Ibid., 70–78.

seven

PHILOSOPHICAL THOUGHTS

> Melancholy persons, with their despondent, secret insides, are potential exiles but also intellectuals capable of dazzling, albeit abstract, constructions.[1]

> *I focus seriously and at great length on things that others are able to let go much sooner. I like words because they can communicate ideas efficiently. I also love blues music because it hypnotizes me and moves me away from myself. I love flowers for the same reason. But I can't understand the meaning of it all. I wasn't built for life, mentally or any other way, or maybe I'm just more honest [than most people].*
>
> *Is the death of innocent children an act of "divine" genocide? Where is the god of mercy and compassion? Our problems are small compared to the real horror, but we like to believe that there is a reason for our suffering, that events are not random, that they occur for a reason. This makes no sense to me, other than that ultimately we would like to know why we suffer. If there wasn't a god, we would have to invent one to blame for our sufferings.*

In her book *The Corporeal Turn*, philosopher Maxine Sheets-Johnstone considers the many desperate efforts of philosophers and theologians to identify the decisive differences between primates and humans, and thus to establish human uniqueness. She finds, however, that differences are of degree only, not of kind.[2] Primates have rationality, the ability to make and use tools, upright posture, etc. In fact, they have some skills that (most) humans do not—like brachiating (swinging from tree limb to tree limb)!

1. Kristeva, *Black Sun*, 64.
2. Sheets-Johnstone, *Corporeal Turn*, 74.

The Wendell Cocktail

All beings' intelligence relates to their surroundings. Humans can't accomplish some intricate and involved things that other species can. We think that because we have built immense structures, we are superior, but as a collective, we are no better than any other species. We have the ability to wage war with weapons of mass destruction; we fight more than most species because we have the weapons. The big-horned mountain goat has its horns to fight with for breeding rights and territory, but they don't fight to kill, only to gain the higher pecking order. I would love to swing through the trees like an orangutan.

Anger is an honest reaction to being alive in this world. There is nothing wrong with feeling angry for real reasons, but it mustn't be allowed to consume you. I often feel guilty about being angry; I have more than a healthy amount of it, coming from my upbringing. I saw how afraid my father was of his anger. It may be easier in the short term to bite your tongue and repress it, but it doesn't work in the long term. Anger is like energy; it can't be destroyed, only transferred to another object, and ultimately, at best, sublimated.

Until we realize that war is childish, not adult behavior, there will always be war. Until we have reached an evolutionary state in which war is outlawed as inhuman, there will always be war. Until we realize that illnesses of the mind are as real and devastating as physical illness, there will always be war. Until we can see blood as pain, and not be excited by it as a shark is, there will be war.

2/17/06

War combines a life of discipline with a life of excess. Discipline has longer-term rewards; excess, shorter. The road to wisdom can come from both, suffering being the common denominator and necessary ingredient. What a life!

We are animals, yet we are unlike other animals in some ways. We pride ourselves on our ideas, but they are of such small scope.

Frequently there are two sides to a story, but sometimes there is only one.

When can logic and faith lie down together like the lion and the lamb: when?

Everything is now, but now is constantly gone; after each word is spoken it's already gone, yesterday.

The young see and understand that there is a huge gap between what is taught and what is done. True intelligence is lost when they become passive and accept the elders' story.

No one, or few, learned from the 1960s. The rebellion led almost all back to the norm, the status quo. Is our generation any different than those of the past? I would say yes, a bit different. Every generation has its own peculiarities which make it somewhat unique. In the 1880s the kids were doing the latest drug, nitrous oxide. This was a university thing, just like marijuana in the 1960s. What has changed? Well, I would say that marijuana is a very different drug in that it has a stimulating, creative effect; it does not tranquilize the creative possibilities. Perhaps some generations need the tranquilizing and some need the hallucinogens.

The green movement is essentially a movement toward minimalism; more people shopping at secondhand stores, more people growing their own food, more choices. With a little time one can find objects of better quality from the past—furniture, cars, and so on. If this trend continues, large corporations will begin to feel the sting. I predict that it will even affect the pharmaceuticals that, until now, hardly anyone is willing to do without.

Just as the years get shorter for old people, as we look back two hundred years or more, we no longer think in terms of a day, a month, or even a year: we order events by decades.

1/21/06

People are not happy when I challenge them about their behavior. Communicate nothing but praise and you'll be okay. But try to stand up for yourself when you have been wronged and they will act as if it is your problem, no apologies, no trying to right the wrong. I have seen it in myself and I have also witnessed it in others.

Once upon a time man as well as beast was under the rule of survival of the fittest. Now we are in a time when the weak are cared for in unprecedented numbers. What will this eventually do to mankind? Will Hitler's fears be realized because we decided on compassion over natural selection? Just asking! I think that Hitler did have valid questions about these issues, although as my mother said, she wouldn't want to be alive in a world where his values were adopted.

eight

RELIGION

THROUGHOUT HIS LIFE THE judgmental fundamentalism of his childhood home was a major target of Wendell's anger. He and I had many conversations in which I tried to convince him that one need not accept our parents' ideas of God. At various times I argued for the process theologians' God: in Dylan Thomas's words, "The force that through the green fuse drives the flower," an energy interior to the world rather than an omnipotent, omniscient ruler/judge. Or I recommended St. Augustine's proposals for how we might fruitfully think of God. In his *On Christian Doctrine* (I.8), he says that "anyone who thinks of God as anything other than life itself has an absurd idea of God." Or, in his homily on 1 John 4:16, Augustine said, "God is love," adding that that is all you need to know about God. Or he called God the "great beauty," saying that the beauty of the world is evidence of the beauty of its creator. I tried to explain to Wendell that all these ways of thinking of God are feeble human efforts to begin to understand so great a mystery, a mystery that human language is ultimately unable to do more than point *toward*.

Wendell was unconvinced. I suspect that, in a perverse way, he *liked* the harsh, judgmental God of his childhood. It/He served the purpose of giving Wendell a focus for his resentment of Christianity.

> *What is the "power of prayer" when our brains cannot even muster enough electricity to power a light bulb? Christians like to believe that prayer has real effects, but I believe that it is action that gets things done, not prayer. Action can move mountains and create "miracles." In Jesus' life, [in order] to change things, he moved around and did things.*

> *Seems fascist to say "just believe" and you will be saved. And they say that God has unconditional love. No, according to them one has to believe in him, to worship him unconditionally; if that isn't a condition, nothing is.*
>
> *The first Christians found empowerment by having a new religion. Strength can come from persecution. It also enables the persecuted to feel more "right," the more others come down on you.*
>
> *Faith means you must go beyond the intelligence you were supposedly given by the deity, an obvious contradiction.*
>
> *For religious people, when things go well it's a "miracle"—God's intervention; when it goes badly, it must be God's will. You can't lose or win; it's all God's will—wonderful when it falls on the positive, not so sweet, but still God's will, when it ends in the negative.*

In the following excerpt, the core of Wendell's bitterness in relation to religion is revealed.

> *I lie awake at night or day and wonder how thinking thoughts can have anything to do with rightness or wrongness. How can a person's honest thoughts become a self-damnation? This seems very oppressive and worrisome to me. Both Catholicism and Protestantism teach that thoughts are dangerous. This takes freedom away from the individual. Christianity wants us to be in this awful predicament. Even though I know this is not right, I still feel that I can't think certain thoughts, even my own private and unsaid thoughts, lest there be consequences. This is partly a product of my mental problems, but it also has to do with the environment of my childhood. Together these made a hell of a team working to destroy me as a person, a human being. I've tried enormously hard to see it their way, but with little effect.*
>
> *The Sunday church crowd: they wear their "getups" and go to the temple. Jesus and God are not on their minds. Many realize that [going to church] will help their income; "networking" is the new word for it. Others truly are trying to be better people, but I would venture to say that church is not the place to find what one seeks. You won't find much when everyone is trying to be nice. This only fills the person's sense of well-being and self. Possibly it may spill over to the following days, but I have not seen much of that and I have spent many years looking. There are no more people in churches that have real love than in any other walk of life. I have no more answers than people of faith, but I have many more questions. Instead, spend your time in the woods; meditate on your life, and use your senses to reach understanding.*

The Wendell Cocktail

I've tried hard to understand and to connect, to attach myself to the truth, but all I've found to be true is the adage, "the more I know, the less I know." I suppose that music is one of the areas that may prove [the existence of] God—music being magic to me, much more than flowers or other sex machines of nature, pre-disposed to perpetuate their species. Music doesn't do anything other than make life more tolerable.

Any time people pray for victory in war, or pray, as I just saw, for successful bull-riding in which animals are abused, or just pray for anything that has nothing to do with healing or goodness, it is taking God's or Jesus' name in vain. It is selfish and stupid to pray for a safe football game, yet you see and hear this all the time. These things are the truly vain, not swearing.

I think that it is equally insane to say that there is no god and that there is a god and to build absolute doctrines around "him"; it's not rational, not scientific.

PART 2

The Last Five Years

nine

2005

IN THE FIVE YEARS preceding his death, Wendell wrote more frequently in his journal, returning again and again to his childhood as the key to his obsessions.

> 4/30
>
> *My father said that it was my "lifestyle" that was to blame for the suffering I experienced. I was trying to be independent. In order to save money I never went out carousing; I never did anything except try to get by the only way I could, which was to paint houses. I knew I could potentially have done better, but this was the best I could do because I had regular panic attacks, high anxiety, and a complete lack of self-esteem.*
>
> *My family does not know at all what I went through during my pre- and post-Ryther Child Center years. If you could only have known the torture I was in, you would have been kinder. The illness caught up with me time and time again. I have had five major depressive episodes, along with ongoing dysthymia (chronic moderate depression). Occasionally I could manage to seem "normal," but mental illness was always there, waiting for a stressful situation which would catapult me into an undignified state, coming apart at the seams. Once when I was so severely depressed that I was wailing and crying, Dad said, "Stand up and act like a man." When Judy, my first girlfriend and lover, rejected me, I completely fell apart. But what many saw as "not being a man about it" was clearly the response of a mentally ill person. But most would rather see it as weakness than as mental illness.*

I asked fair, intelligent questions about the cosmos and Dad called me a blasphemer. Right up to the end of his life, I could do nothing to please him. He never could deal "outside the box," and was always offended by any other "powers" that were—MDs, theologians with differing views. And that is all it is!—views, theories, opinions. We don't know—can't know. I often witnessed his animosity, not just toward me, but toward anyone who challenged him in the slightest. Oh sure, he got along fabulously with those who agreed with him.

I don't know if he loved or hated me, but with his actions he made me feel like a rotten little boy.

3/7

Dad always said that he was too busy with "the Lord's work" to attend to my needs as a baby/little boy/man. But he chose with free will, as he liked to say, where to put his energy. He never bonded with me. This was an adult's responsibility, not a small boy's prerogative.

3/8

Margi once related a story about when I was a wee thing. She was pushing me in the stroller across the Fremont Bridge, and she says that she thought about throwing me off the bridge. I realize that she never would have, and it was told with a sense of humor, but with all humor, revelations are revealed. I realize that my sisters, as well as my dad, resented me. Margi told me on several occasions that I was a "mistake," which doesn't bother me except that I see how that fits in with my dad's behavior; possibly I was a reminder of his uncontrolled lust? The real horror now is to know that my sisters think I will suicide and they do nothing about it.

I imagine you as you read my thoughts, thinking: he's lost, immature. Possibly, but I've done my goddamn best. I am who I am, and I would never want to live without the ability to be discerning, wondering, questioning. People like me are useful to society, no matter how painful it is for us.

Clinging to straws and falling down define my waking life. All my potential talent is wasted. Maybe I could have been a philosopher or a photographer. All I know is that I think constantly, no respite, no peace. I could do without the answers if I could only have peace. All I ever asked from God was peace. I never wanted a big house, cars, and money—I only asked and asked again and again for a sense of rightness and peace.

3/21

Since I wake up every day it seems I need to do things to make myself feel better, like smoking and drinking.

I found a way to extend my life. I never could have made it this far if I hadn't found pain relief, both physical and mental. But now the relief is diminishing. This goes back many years to my youth. I feel that I have been courageous; only I know how much suffering I've been through. I am just very tired of the 10 percent of the time that I am "okay" and the 90 percent that I am not. And that wonderful half of 1 percent when I feel bliss. I know enough now not to strive for that now, just some kind of peace would do.

I no longer have long-term plans, but it makes sense for the short term that I try to stop smoking and drinking, for awhile at least. I will smell and taste things better, not have to hack up vile-looking phlegm. Trying to protect themselves from this dirty smoke, my lungs build up mucous. Also, I have shortness of breath, especially in the morning; I get panicked about it.

3/28

I'm having a hard time moving my head without spasm. "What you see is what you get." What I get is to live, to try hard against the demands of a relentless illness, and then die with little understanding or acknowledgment.

Time heals all wounds? No, with time a scab forms, and the scab never disappears.

5/25

In 1999 I was trying to get to know my dad. I went to his home every year for seven to ten days for about five years.

ten

2006

Now WENDELL IS THINKING through the case for ending a painful life. He considers his mother's death, finding it unnecessarily extended, her suffering aggravated and prolonged by her doctors' refusal to end suffering that could not possibly have any other outcome than death. He seeks values that transcend the value of prolonging life. His angers deepen. Returning to old themes, he rehearses arguments to support bringing his ever-increasing pain to an end.

> 2/15
>
> *I think that the faithful can't afford a quiet mind, any more than I can with my challenges. This is where the culture of religion comes in: surround yourself with those who believe as you do—precariously, tenuously; this is what will help to dissipate doubt. Not a very courageous way to embrace life. The mind is governed by fear; its radar is always searching for the threat. I must not allow myself to be eaten, it repeats to itself as a mantra; instead, I must eat.*
>
> *What do we really know? But we walk carelessly as if we know, the horror close behind, nipping at our heels like a blind person who doesn't know what's in front. We are nervous, tentative, but can never afford to admit it. We are closed-minded out of fear.*
>
> *One person uses words to harm others; another person uses violence. In either case, harm is done.*
>
> *I get up at night to watch stars and planets. Last night and tonight Jupiter will be visible in the northeast. It glistens because of the cold atmosphere on earth, with every color in the spectrum. Really makes one long to have some small part of the self immortal.*

10/20

What's wrong with feeling you've lived long enough and having the means to say, "up to here and no further?" I watched as Mother went from eating a little, to not eating, to being unconscious; [we didn't know] whether she was in pain. The doctors said that she was not in pain, but I stayed with her a couple of nights, changing her diapers and hearing her moans. So I went to the doctor and he gave me only one suppository that I had to stick up her anus. It seemed to make no difference. She spent six weeks in a totally helpless state. Mother had a very undignified death, and I think there is little or no excuse for it. How can this be forgiven? When she died my father gave the bulk of his—and my mother's—money to people he did not know: missionaries and students on the fast track to "saving souls."

"It's in God's hands" is one of the dumbest things I've ever heard. This answer is given by people dying of AIDS in Africa when they are asked to teach their children how to avoid AIDS. "It's in God's hands" is an excuse to avoid doing the right thing. We are responsible, we make decisions all the time that affect whether people live or die, or are maimed in some way. When it comes to death, it is not "in God's hands," it is the family's decision whether a tube is pulled or a cord is yanked. Life is not all that precious; it is arrogant to assume so. It's rather a "dime a dozen." I have never wanted [to be judgmental]; I want to be an understanding person, but these things are unfathomable to me. All I ever saw was pain and dysfunction. Once my mom was only a shell, at least then, with all the medical abilities we have, she should have been released, but everyone was too afraid to tamper.

A hundred years from now I think that no one will need to suffer pain. Perhaps people will be put in a coma until their injuries are healed. Most of us are in a state of suspended animation or quiet desperation anyway. But is pain necessary to prompt compassion? Some can handle certain kinds of pain—physical or mental—much better than others. Physical pain is easy for me. I can go through it, knowing it will end at a certain point. Mental pain is another sort of demon; one never knows when it will end, nor what is causing it. One cannot, in that state, have any confidence in relief.

I'm self-effacing, insecure mentally and spiritually, distressed, selfish at times when I am overwhelmed by my illness, angry. But I am also polite, caring, and passionate, especially about the suffering of all beings. I have a very good eye for things, love all natural beings and feel compassion for them. I am usually fairly passive, but if someone is rude to me, then I lash out. I think too much, I know. I

The Wendell Cocktail

really have to try to differentiate between the things that annoy me in this town and the drugs that affect me.

It's one thing to end your life when you have not tried to seek help—professional help, spiritual help, or mental help. It's another thing to judge the act and avoid seeing how desperately the person has sought and suffered. The therapists say that there is always hope, but they do not see the real. There are people and times that do not fit in the "saved plan." If they were honest they would have to admit that some lives are beyond hope and to help those people release themselves. I never imagined that I would ever be fifty-six years old, and I am tired and sick. I have had enough of life. I will miss the beauty, but the pain is always with me. Please remember my past and don't judge me. I have gone through a lot of psychotherapy, and it has helped me to some degree. I only ask that, like me, you seek to understand, not only to give yourself a sense of peace, but to find the truth of a person's life—my life.

It's the light we fear; the darkness is unconsciousness, so-called "rest in peace." Peace is a living concept. The living cannot or do not want to accept the nothingness that existed before we were born. I know that I have little to offer now. I do my best to have my heart in the best place, but I know that money is the only real thing I have left. My ability to save money, pitiful as it is, has left me with some options. Failure has been my only other companion.

In 1994 when I was going through a major severe depression I was taken to a private psychiatric clinic in Kirkland. I was admitted, but I grew afraid and claustrophobic when big doors locked behind me. So I changed my story so I could get out. Staying at the clinic would have wiped my money out, since I had no psychiatric insurance, and if there's one thing I couldn't handle it would be becoming a slave to work again in order to survive. All I have is my ability to avoid working for someone else. I keep myself insulated, at least to the extent of not having the further humiliation of having to be a yes-man.

Everything I am makes sense to me much of the time. Self-deception doesn't work for me, so I live with a strong sense of awareness. I don't know how I've lived so long. I feel fortunate for what I have (materially). I worked hard for it, and I could not have! I could have not struggled in my earlier years, but one strong incentive was to achieve independence at all costs. Every day I feared that my work would not continue another day so I worked and saved, thinking any day could be my last.

Across my thoughts with nets of curiosity
I chase the translucent butterfly of God

We think of death as natural. Nevertheless, we're afraid of death. But we seldom think about the intolerable suffering that precedes it. At age twelve I was in so much mental anguish that I couldn't see at the time how one person could suffer so much without the world being aware—a twelve-year-old's ignorance.

My only coping mechanism is hypervigilance, that is, paranoia. Yet I also try to be sensitive. I'm so tired. I never knew I would live this long; I never wanted to. Since Ryther I have coped in many ways, trying to find a smooth road. But I realize now that I never had the variety of coping mechanisms others had.

When one is treated with insults and jeers, one doesn't respond with pleasantness. My father always insulted my intelligence and gave me no personal respect. Is it any wonder that I either put men on pedestals or hate them?

I wish I could feel love for you all, imperfect as I know you would call yourselves. "Imperfect" doesn't accurately describe your behavior. When you are going to sleep the things I've described must hound you; if they don't, they should.

I waver between trying to believe in a god and not believing at all. Had I more confidence in myself I would probably lean toward the latter. The founding fathers said that we, the people, should not be subject to tyranny. I think that includes trying to make people conform to an ideology; that's tyranny and hostility at its core. People seek to convince themselves of a belief system by trying to convince others. If they can persuade others, their own beliefs are reinforced. Let's leave the hate generated by beliefs and [go for] loving behavior.

I have a willow tree I started as a twig, and now it is eight years old. It's trying to weep because it's a weeping willow but it's too young as yet. It will need to get older before it can weep. It is still growing, reaching for the sky. When it gets older it will learn to weep.

I need a soft, gentle asylum, especially now. I need a place to hide. Sanctuary, asylum, refuge, retreat, backing off from the usual activities, safe from all who would harm. Asylum: a place where help can be given. Refuge: danger is close by, but short-term safety is at hand.

If there is anything beyond our conscious life it certainly is not determined by what a person believes, but by how you behaved while alive. No one is perfect, but when you have wronged someone you have to admit it and apologize. This is all there is, so simple yet so difficult.

eleven

2007

In 2007 Wendell reviewed his life obsessively, fantasizing about death, reliving the beauty and the pain, the good times and the bad. His journal entries no longer seem random. Rather, they gather and build, focusing on the themes of his earlier journals—family, nature, animals, the pains and the pleasures of his life—considering, seeing whether the objects to which he is minutely attentive *hold* or if they attenuate and evaporate in the anguish of his memories.

I have included several quotations from Pascal and other authors to demonstrate Wendell's remarkable similarity of thought. To my knowledge, he never read Pascal or the others I quote.

> *If you were in a volcano and knew you were about to die, and you had a deadly weapon with you, would you allow yourself to be burned or would you shoot yourself? All these do-gooders believe that "it's all in God's hands," which is a real error. So either one must end in agonizing death, or when it is known to be coming, to shoot yourself in order to have a better exit. However, ten grams of Seconal would be the best exit.*
>
> *If you take your life into your own hands, then you must evaluate what is important; you have no one else to rely on. Do you want a big house, car, and/or children you want to show off? Do you want to spend your life working at something you hate so you can maintain an image? What will be your "image" when you are (so soon) rotting in the grave? This is life: to live and to die. So hard for humanity at this point in time; so we make up fantasies to help us deal with the sting. Don't ask me why I can't accept it, or if you ask me I will, in humility, give you my ideas. Dignity at or near the end [depends on] Seconal.*

The right to life should also imply the right to death. Perhaps the rest home lobbies and the pharmaceuticals are behind the lack of [legislation] permitting a person to end their life. Lots of money can be made on the sick! I don't believe in conspiracy theories; it's more a matter of unconnected but like-minded individuals in the quest for money. I mainly just wonder, always wondering, the main saga of my life.

No one can take responsibility for another's life, just for one's own. When a person chooses to say that he has had enough of life it should at least be accepted, if not respected. People should be able to do as they choose as long as others are not intentionally hurt. None of us, no matter how good, can completely avoid unintentional hurt to others.

My depression has always prevented me from having an awakening, seeing with fresh eyes, pondering with delight. But perhaps I've always seen things as they are, both the loveliness of the earth and its horrors.

Seems to me that someone or something as powerful as God could easily make an appearance as a father would, saying: "Now, you kids have had a free rein, but I have to step in now to correct you!" That sounds like a real father: strong, good, caring, and loving. But if there is a God I just don't understand why he/she/it would leave us totally alone.

Curiosity is the key to all intelligence. I can't help being curious because it's who I am, as much a part of me as my face.

My hope is to die with some sort of spiritual confidence. I don't believe in "the spiritual"—a name attached to man's fantasy, blind faith. But I am as open as I can be, with my particular brain chemistry and intelligence. I do pray and ask for help in terms of understanding, I always have, but in all honesty I have to preface my prayer with: "if you exist, God." I cannot pray in any other way; I can't fake it. If there is an all-knowing God it would be the first to understand my mind, and faking it would be absurd.

We are born with a sex sickness that is completely separate from rationality. We foolishly think that lust is love. But does it come from the heart or from the loins? Are we just intelligent monkeys? And why does so-called love often turn to vile hatred? I have wondered why my father allowed me to read The Scarlet Letter *when I was fourteen. I think that he wanted me to be aware of his own temptations.*

Dad was suspicious of me because he was suspicious of himself and knew what a penis could do. But he never told me anything about sex, except when I was fifteen, he remarked to me, "It only takes once!" I had no idea what he was referring to.

God versus gods: was a single god rather than many merely a way to make our life simpler? If you make a person of faith defensive you will get hate. Challenge my beliefs and I will tear you to pieces— very loving, eh? I think I would be open to anything as long as it made sense, but that is just the problem; nothing has made sense.

Everyone wants an anchor. The problem is, there isn't one. I would like nothing more than an anchor that would keep me in one place. Adrift; we are all riders on the storm. I, like others, would like to think there is help outside of myself. Please convince me; this is my humble prayer. I will be humble; I will kneel down; I will lie down, but I cannot say I think something that I don't think.

We burn with desire to find a firm footing, an ultimate, lasting base on which to build a tower reaching up to infinity, but our whole foundation cracks and the earth opens up into the depths of the abyss.[1]

I often have to reconstruct myself on an hourly basis. I don't think anyone realizes just how strenuous this is.

I have become an alcoholic and drug-dependent person, the only way I can deal with life. I don't think it makes me a bad person, but it does alter my perspective. I have always been depressed and I have never been able to overcome it. So the only way I could find relief from my mind was to take mind-altering drugs. I fought [alcohol and drugs] successfully until Mother died, then I began to give up. I've constantly thought of death since I was eleven or twelve when I had my first breakdown, my first major depressive episode. I don't know what to do anymore other than rely on chemicals to get me through the day. If I had my way I would want to sleep all the time—so unlike how I felt when I was in my twenties and early thirties, but very like where I was when I was eleven or twelve. I just remember wanting to be "out of it." I didn't want to die, but I wanted to be asleep for several days. This is how painful it was for me. Not a spoiled kid trying to get attention, but a deeply disturbed kid. This is when I went to Ryther Child Center. I remember one man, probably in his mid-twenties, working on his master's degree, who took a liking to me. That's what I needed: a male model, just a friend who cared. He has made some difference in my perception of men.

---

1. Pascal, *Pensées*, # 199.

2007

The only reason I'm still here is because of my mother's love. It was imperfect, but it was real and deep and it made a difference. If I had a different mother, I certainly would be dead or in jail and I wouldn't have the side of myself that is sweet. My mother was very sweet, always putting herself to the side for the sake of others. I miss her so much that I can barely get through some days. I've never felt anything as close to anyone as we were. I think of how she worked to make Christmas a magical event; of the help she gave me when I was trying to get my painting business going; of the kindness she showed when I was so very lost; of the love she showed my girlfriends. They only had to be near me for her to show them nonjudgmental kindness. Mother never had a mean streak in her body or mind. Maybe she felt things she didn't show, but as sensitive as I am, I never picked up on anything.

"Bridge Over Troubled Water": we listened to that song over and over and she truly loved it with me. It meant so much for her to connect with me on that. But my father always came and told us to turn it down. Any connection I had with my mom bothered my dad greatly. He seemed to hate to hear my mom and me having a good time; he was jealous of his son—sick but true. Thinking about those times makes me want to go crazy or die.

"You shall know them by their fruits"; Dad had fruits for strangers but not for his wife and children. He was the classic go-out-and-perform, and then come home and be himself; he was not a kind, gentle, lenient, guiding parent. My mother took all the burden of raising us, and even took on a job at the age of fifty-five or so as a librarian at the University of Washington, working until she was sixty-five. Mary Lillian Brown. God, I love my mama; I can barely write without breaking down. Yet what a shitty son I was. Only in the last years of her life was I able to be almost an adult. Of course I was only thirty-five when she died. I never had a chance to become an adult with her because she was forty-three when I was born and I was an immature person well into my thirties.

Simply put, I think I got my dad's anger and my mother's sweetness, and both my dad's and mom's anxiety.

We build and we are busy as an avoidance technique.

What people want is not the easy peaceful life that allows us to think of our unhappy condition, nor the dangers of war, nor the burdens of office, but the agitation that takes our mind off it and diverts it. That is why we prefer the hunt to the capture.[2]

---

2. Ibid., #136.

The Wendell Cocktail

Romantic lustful love makes both parties look the other way. The truth is not in view because this feels too good. Until my lust fails I won't take a good look at the truth that we really have little or nothing in common. We did not ask for these hormones that make us go crazy! We can't transcend this sexual need; will power is fruitless; we are coitus machines, though some of us manage to merge lust with love.

If I had been born with a heart defect, everyone would not only understand but be sympathetic. I know no one will ever understand my mental condition. Since I am reasonably intelligent most of the time, others are not willing to [acknowledge] that I deserve the same sympathy as people with cancer. Maybe a hundred years from now . . .

Question Christian culture and you will be in hell on earth; you will be ostracized. You will feel it and know it. No room for questions. But I now know that there are many people who think as I do, who cannot choose either belief or atheism. This is the hardest spot to be in. Atheists can find like minds; religious people can find like minds. But maintaining a position of openness and searching is more difficult. To be in this world alone, without answers, is a position I would not wish on anyone, but it is the only honest way for me. It is me at my core. I think people will accept any theology in order to no longer be an outsider. Most of the desire [to believe] comes from the need to be accepted.

The stresses of being in the woods really show you who you are. In a primitive place, the primitive mind also rears its ancient, ugly head. In all the human centuries we have barely budged from our beginning, some 100,000 years ago.

Before Mother died my fantasy was to own a house where I could live on one level and Mother and Dad could live on another, and I could take care of them. But Mom died and Dad got a new wife and that shot that plan. The fantasy was that I could come home and talk with my mom and help her when she needed it. I think it would have made me a better man. I realize that I would also want to be separate; that is why two levels were important. I think I could have pulled it off, but I never could have with my dad and a new wife.

I have a weird combination of intelligence and addiction. The intelligent side and the addictive side are constantly at war. In the night I spend my waking hours thinking of all the bad stuff, and during the day I have to be chemically altered in order to survive, to have a modicum of relief from BNM—back, neck, mind.

Everyone likes to hear about the weak side of Wendell; it makes them feel stronger, more in control, caring. Sometimes, often, my mind feels like a tornado, racing in a circle; it can't stop.

We can't handle being alone, even in beautiful surroundings; we seem to thrive on distraction. Even Buddhist monks who don't converse have each other's company. Everything else is just an elaborate cultural distraction, bent on perpetuating the species and its current ideologies. Very few people could handle even a few days of doing nothing. Try living for three days on nothing, as I did—no food, no water, just the woods and a busy mind—then you can say that you know something.

Anyone who does not see the vanity of the world is very vain himself. So who does not see it, apart from young people whose lives are all noise, diversions, and thoughts for the future? But take away their diversion and you will see them bored to extinction. Then they feel their nullity without recognizing it. Nothing could be more wretched than to be intolerably depressed as soon as one is reduced to introspection with no means of diversion.[3]

We often think of a person who says one thing at one time, and another at another time, as being a hypocrite, a phony, but [it also might be that] some people are open to learning and are willing to change their opinions.

Goodness, weakness, and meanness: these can all be attributes of the same person. We all have fear, weakness, and the need to be a "good person." When we feel fear we sometimes lash out from sheer frustration, lack of composure, and it's easier to be mean than to find intelligent words. Poor humans; look at the childish behavior everywhere. It should be considered a crime to go to war, yet we ourselves all have a war going on within us. We distract ourselves from it by lashing out at others rather than dealing with our own wars.

My heart is pure but my brain is damaged. I knew a guy with muscular dystrophy who could barely talk, but he graduated from college. Most of my peers thought it very uncool to be with a "spaz" but I liked this guy as I liked anyone who was willing to talk to me. Sure, I felt sorry for him, but I should probably have felt sorry for myself instead.

---

3. Ibid., #36.

The Wendell Cocktail

If you feel guilty, you will probably also cause others to feel guilty; oppressive guilt is a product of abuse, and we know that the abused more often than not become the abuser.

I'm frustrated with people who don't work and could. I had mental illness and a broken neck and back and I was out there busting my ass trying to make a living, so it's one area I'm not very tolerant. I can't understand it; I think it goes beyond laziness, but maybe there are issues of which I am unaware. I know that if you dig deeply, things are usually not black-and-white, but this work thing really gets my goat, as Dorothy would say. I'm not talking about those who can't work, not even remotely, as my disabled nephew Randy would say. Randy is a beautifully sensitive man. He understands emotional and physical pain; what a gift to have him in my life.

Some like to make war, some like to watch it. People are not happy in peace. We have a deep, primal interest in war and violence.

Sometimes, when I think about the various activities of men, the dangers and troubles which they face at court, or in war, giving rise to so many quarrels and passions, daring and often wicked enterprises and so on, I have often said that the sole cause of man's unhappiness is that he does not know how to sit quietly in his room.[4]

Can you imagine trying to act "normal" when you feel a screwdriver being pressed into your spine? Not necessarily a ten on the pain scale, but a chronic five spot.

9/11 [Wendell's 57th birthday]

Since life may be short for me, I want to leave my property in good shape, painted and pretty, lawns cut, and gardens weeded, so the next owner will be happy. Today I sprayed the two sides of my house that take the weather. It took a lot out of me and caused a great deal of pain, so I know I have to wait several days to do the trim work. It's important to me to keep my place up. The clutter in my head, my "voice," says, hey man, keep your place clean and pretty and I will leave you alone (but it never does). Certain psychopathologies have no cure (like cancer in the body). When will we ever learn? Perhaps our genetic makeup prevents us from learning the most important things.

---

4. Ibid, #136.

2007

I made a bust in ceramics class in 1968. I had it for a few years until it got lost. But over the last five or ten years I have realized, from the picture of it I have, that it is quite similar to my appearance now—same hair, facial features, and mustache. It's kind of weird to think that I made an image of myself forty years before I became that image.

Me: A few marbles missing at birth and then an environment that rattles the remaining marbles. Music was a small salvation from age seven on. Science is now becoming important, though not with my childlike passion toward music and growing things. I almost always experience either excitement or deep depression; possibly I have not been diagnosed properly.

Each generation thinks they are special, and every generation has some need to go through something, a rite of passage. The boomer generation felt they had to put themselves through fire "spiritually" by taking LSD and other drugs; our fathers' fire was World War II.

We know many things that we don't think about because we can't do anything about them. For example, it is dangerous to be alive on this planet because of the natural radiation prevalent in our atmosphere; there is no escape for the living.

September 28: This is the first day since June 5 that I've needed to buy a vegetable; I still have four or five cantaloupes and plenty of broccoli and carrots, and have tomatoes for another week or more. I think with a greenhouse I could extend all of these things by two months. I ate my last peppers but still have yellow crookneck zucchini.

The lives of the ancients must have been very different in terms of perceptions of time. I don't think we can even imagine it. Time must have gone by much more slowly when physical needs did not require enormous effort. There must have been much more time for contemplation, silence, except for the sounds of nature, animals, and wind. It sounds like heaven to me because I require a good deal of quiet. I am as afraid of too much quiet as anyone, but I'm trying to learn to embrace the frightening aspect of being alone. But every age had its limitations. We think we have so much more now; yes, more artificial stimulation, driven by corporate values. We work our asses off for more and more, but we get less and less in the process.

The threatening existential condition is acted out in the pursuit of more, . . . [signifying] an anxious emptiness covered over with never-ending fulfillments.[5]

---

5. Sheets-Johnstone, *Roots of Morality*, 380.

The Wendell Cocktail

It isn't that I love trees and animals because they don't talk back. They do; they are just so much gentler, softer in their responses; to hear them requires a quiet within oneself, even a darkness or sadness. They can also be dangerous; an animal may bite or a tree may fall. But I have always felt that I would rather take my chances with the wilds than with the sophisticated, cunning, manipulative ways of humans which confuse and confound me and pain my little brain.

Life is boredom, occasionally broken by beauty, peace, involvement; seeing other species and our own in different states of being, sometimes wonderful, sometimes horrible, and panic always lurking at the sidelines, waiting to attack.

Being unable to cure death, wretchedness, and ignorance, men have decided, in order to be happy, not to think about these things. Despite these afflictions man wants to be happy, only wants to be happy, and cannot help wanting to be happy.[6]

When I went to the emergency room with my decapitated finger I realized that one is terrifically vulnerable in any state of need. The doctors, nurses, and police that are present must enjoy their position of power. After all, they are in control. If they perceive you to be a person of less worth, or one who questions their status, you will be treated differently. It may be quite unconscious but I've been in states of both physical and mental vulnerability many times, and being sensitive I think I have a fairly accurate estimation of people. Oh, I forgot to mention "counselors" and the clergy—very much the same thing. These people must have deference; otherwise, abuse is just around the corner.

People try to feed off me, even though I earned my money the hard way; it really offends me. I painted houses and spent countless hours in the library trying to find investments that had a good risk/reward ratio. The little I make on those investments barely gets me by.

Good luck, all of you, on your fantastical "spiritual journey." You think you're right while all the others are wrong. I don't think anyone is right except as it works for you. That is, if it helps, use it, but don't expect some afterlife. When you're dead, you're dead; if you have any contradicting information I'd like to hear it, but please don't use the same old sufferings that you cling to now to argue that there must be an afterlife reward. You rely on a two-thousand-year-old religious history founded by a bunch of bigoted scribes who wrote the bible long after Jesus tried to get his message across—I mean,

---

6. Pascal, *Pensées*, #133, #134.

come on! We have little or no knowledge of Jesus except when he became a radical.

All my life when I prayed to an uncertain god I asked only that I would be given a tidbit of truth. But always the answer was a big zero. I fasted several times, including three days in the woods without food or water; I barely made it out. I was a stupid, ignorant kid, and I don't think I'm any wiser now. I so wish I could believe; why can't I? My entire life has been filled with angst; at fifty-seven I feel completely used up. I hate to get up in the morning, yet I do. I go through the same motions, but because life makes little sense it's getting harder by the day. My own life feels like a stupid mistake and all I can see most of the time is the horror, and my thoughts seem to be unsupported by those around me.

I was an alcoholic in my early twenties; then I was able to quit, drinking only occasionally until I was forty-three; that's when I gave up mentally and physically. My back and neck were in such pain that I don't know which was worse; they were intermingled. At that time I gave up. I lived in my van for four months, totally alone and freaking out. Yet I did not seek help because by then I realized that no one I turned to would be able to help. By then I had spent time at the Ryther Child Center and with numerous psychiatrists and clinical therapists, getting little or no real help. I had also sought out Christians that I thought would help, but that was even more depressing and devastating. So the last fifteen years of my life I have resorted to drugs. I couldn't have gotten this far without them. I've paid a price, but I still believe that without drugs I would not have even gotten to this point.

10/26

I would like to be on a small ranch (20 acres) with a vineyard and fruit trees, with a half-acre garden sufficient to feed me all year round. And since I'm dreaming, it would be on the coast above Pt. Reyes. Plenty of time to love the birds and animals, and plenty of time to sow and nurture my garden. Two freezers to get me though the winter and time to ride leisurely on an old mare with my dog, riding on the beach at sunset. I do have some of these things right now. I can replace a freezer that a renter stole from me, and I could always get an old mare to ride. But here the growing season is too short by several months. In the Bay Area you can even have two crops of many, but not all, vegetables.

When I was eighteen or so, I was idealistic but I was also angry. I suppressed the anger in favor of trying to be good. But life and alcohol brought out the real me, which was very angry, the result of a father that hated me. I did the best I could, trying to be loving and understanding, but it just took a bit of alcohol to bring out the angry Wendell. My father hated what I was, a boy growing up who was loved by his mother. Dad hated me because Mother used me to protect her from sex with my father, whom she didn't love. How can a boy survive as a pawn between two adults?

I just want soft asylum in my mind, but I can't believe that anything of the sort will come. Perhaps a sanctuary like the church I used to visit after my hike at St. Edwards State Park. I'd sit in a pew and pray, but no peace came. Christians say, "You must be doing something wrong." If I am it's because my mind doesn't work like theirs; it's not that I'm any less worthy; my mind has never been able to embrace their form of understanding. I'm not alone, but I feel that way because I haven't been able to meet people like me in this town, though I know they are plentiful everywhere in the world.

I stopped fishing because I started feeling the fishes' pain. I could see their breathing becoming shallower and I thought of their suffering. That sensitivity has a lot to do with my own suffering. I find it easier to eat supermarkets' kill; because I don't see the suffering, I can detach from it. But now I cannot kill fish or animals even though I participate in their killing because I eat their packaged meat.

The spark plugs are still firing here, but more and more sluggishly; my car and I are both becoming sluggish. I need new plugs or something to keep me going. My entire life has been this way.

Your only hope is to work the good in you; try not to allow the "bad" to take over the good.

Mother said, "When you were in such immense pain I heard you call on Jesus." Maybe I did, but the point is, in desperation we will always call on the unattainable. When the pain is great, you would call out to a dog if you thought that it might help.

Conservatives are all for protecting the unborn child, yet they are very willing to send young women and men to their deaths in wars. They also argue against euthanasia with complete arrogance and insensitivity toward the suffering of people who don't want to live anymore. Does it make sense to save the lives of those who don't want to live, and allow the "unborn" to be killed when they reach the delicate age of eighteen years old?

11/6

One's ethics are dramatically compromised when one has no financial resources. We need money, and ethics should be more important in proportion to the amount of money one has. But this is not the case.

twelve

2008

Every time I have had a major clinical depression episode lasting from four to nine months (and I have had five), I feel like a part of my brain was destroyed. Now that there's not a lot left to work with, I lose "willpower." My minor addictions have turned major, though this may also result from age.

The difference between science and religion: science says we don't know and we want to find out. Religion says we know and we don't want to find out anything else.

Some think that poverty creates a badly behaved person. Society is all too quick to prejudge everyone. Make an inappropriate statement, or be fat or ugly or poor, and you quickly become a forgettable person.

I think I know Jesus but not in Christian terms; I think I know Muhammad and Buddha. But when it comes down to fighting through my anguish, I get no help. I also thought that information would be my salvation, but it probably would eventually boil down to blind faith, of which I am incapable.

I have a right to have a brain that wonders and questions things, and I think that I also have a right as a human being to a sense of anger and frustration that I can't seem to come up with the answers I need. I don't expect to know everything, but it would be nice to have an inkling of some of the answers.

When I see the blind and wretched state of man, when I survey the whole universe in its dumbness and man left to himself with no light, as though lost in this corner of the universe, without knowing who put him there, what he has come to do, what will become of him when he dies, incapable of knowing anything, I am moved to terror, like a man transported in his sleep to some terrifying desert island, who wakes up quite lost and with no means of escape. Then I marvel that so wretched a state does not drive people to despair. I see other people around me, made like myself. I ask them if they are any better informed than I, and they say that they are not. Then these lost and wretched creatures look around and find some attractive objects to which they become addicted and attached. For my part, I have never been able to form such attachments, and considering how very likely it is that there exists something besides that which I can see, I have tried to find out whether God has left any traces of himself.[1]

The simpler I can make my life, the more time I have to do the things I like to do: walk in the woods, photography, plants. But for planting I need good soil, which means I have the complication of adding manure. The best thing I can do is to compost; that simplifies my life. I'd love to have solar panels and vegetable oil to simplify and make my life cheaper; giving me more time to be free.

We think we're all so great, so morally wonderful, different from those who steal and kill. But if we had had the same circumstances, we would no doubt be the same.

Nothing human is alien to me.[2]

Theory, religion, philosophy is for the rich and idle. Average people spend their time trying to put food on the plate. If time to think is based on economic prosperity so that only the rich and idle can really think, we are doomed.

When I die all you suckers can fake sadness, but it will be you that have to live the rest of your lives with whatever illusions you have created to make your life tolerable. I already know that my life has been sustained by chemicals and I'm sad for that, but they have been the "enablers" that twelve-steppers talk about. Don't judge my life, just try to understand that there is more to survival than the illusions you have created for yourselves.

I saw my next-door neighbors laughing as I had a bad spill and cracked my head and back on the ice. I have tried to help when I saw an eighty-year-old woman struggling up the driveway; I came out to ask Maggie to stop barking when I saw her. Jesus asks people to

1. Pascal, *Pensées*, #198.
2. Terence, *Heauton Timorumenos* (*The Self-Torturer*).

love each other—is this too much to ask? I think that this is the only standard that could make us different from the animals or, I should say, non-human animals. We think we're so wonderful, yet we carry chips the size of a cord of wood on our shoulders. This is the cause of wars; Jesus and others with insight tried to tell this was wrong. Love your neighbors and your enemies as you love yourself, he said.

This is a big order, but it may be the only hope for mankind. It makes both the other and oneself feel better. These actions on a global scale could solve the problems of the world. But as long as there is competitiveness, pride, ego, and, just like other animals, territorial aggressiveness, it will never happen.

Some Christians love the idea that the world is coming to an end (whatever that means); they think that then they will be ecstatic while everyone else will be burning in hell. How ridiculous to believe that God is love and that a loving God would act in this way, not based on what you do, but on what you believe. Most Christians only know how to judge, to point out other people's errors, while they think that they will be taken to this fantasyland of heaven just because they said, "we believe" in the their minds—how ridiculous.

I've been to the mountaintops—literally. I've been through the woods and mountains, thirty-five miles in, when no one would have ever been able to help me had I had an accident there. If there is a so-called spirit, that's where it would be found. I've been fortunate to have been to all these wonderful places. They are not permanent; they haven't always been there, and they will change in a manner that no one can anticipate. Maybe another cold or hot time will occur, in which trees and foliage all disappear.

More things are learnt in the woods than in books. Animals, trees, and rocks teach you things not to be heard elsewhere.[3]

I am consumed with whether I will see my mother again. I'm going to visit Mother's grave to see if I can feel any of her spirit, any at all. I know I won't have a long dying with Mother and my friends by my side. I've made my bed, now I'll have to die in it. I will either go by the gun or by Seconal. Please forgive me. My life is mine, and I've had my share of pain. Don't ask me to go through the lingering death my mother went through.

All these things have been on my mind since I was sixteen. I may never have peace, but I know I'll be all right if there is some

---

3. Bonaventure, *Mind's Road to God*, 10.

big cosmic master. Did you miss anything before you were born? Of course not; same with death.

Oh, the horrors that were, and are. Is death the only release? If I'm not doing something physical my mind never stops racing. Even in dreams the horrors continue. I wake up feeling that I've been through a tunnel in hell.

Imagine a number of men in chains, all under sentence of death, some of whom are each day butchered in the sight of the others; those remaining see their own condition in that of their fellows, and looking at each other with grief and despair await their turn. This is an image of the human condition.[4]

I'm sick of the lies, the pretenses, the sickness in our family and in the world. I have nothing to live for. I've tried to help people with money or labor; then I find out they already have plenty of help. I'm sick of people who never do as they say they will. I'm all alone. I wake up in a panic every morning realizing that I have no one—no mother, no friends who care about me, no one. My whole life is screwed up because of a mental illness that began in childhood. It has affected my life tremendously. My sisters don't like me. The women I've loved behave like my father. I'm ready to check out. I spend my day trying desperately to find a reason to live, but other than my dog, Maggie, I can find none. I'm not hungry anymore; I have to force myself to eat. This is no way to live. I've lost every friend I have because I've distanced myself from them.

I'm getting less interested in what others think; they're so predictable, and the files in their brains don't stay open for new thoughts.

4/20

When I close my eyes and squint in a certain way I can see people's faces; it only lasts a second or so, but I don't know why it started a couple of years ago. I've seen Jim Morrison, Jesus, many unknown faces. I love when it happens.

Man's plunder of the earth began in the 1880s with the oil needed to sustain the machines by which the world was becoming a society of the very rich and the very poor. By the 1950s and '60s a middle class was created, but at this point, things have begun to reverse and we have become a world of rich and poor again. The middle class is dying out. The rat race continues, but now the rats

---

4. Pascal, *Pensées*, # 434.

have become meaner, more malicious. They will bite you as soon as you turn your back. It gets harder all the time as political and corporate [businesses] will take more than their fair share.

When I die, you'll still be living a life of self-deception based on your religion—sad. You'll still be playing the game, and I'll be gone, but not to see my mama as I wish. There's nothing I want more than that, but I'm afraid it's all a hoax. No way to prove it. Only a bunch of scribes that wanted to set up a political power, which is all that belief is. I would have loved to believe as they do, but my mind with all its questions could not embrace it, not from pride, but from humility. We know nothing, yet we think, in our little tunnel perspective, that we can know everything. This just comes from fear. I really have trouble with people who say they believe and never question!

It is therefore quite certainly a great evil to have . . . doubts, but it is at least an indispensible obligation to seek when one does thus doubt; so the doubter who does not seek is at the same time very unhappy and very wrong. I do not know who put me into the world, nor what the world is, nor what I am myself. I am terribly ignorant about everything. I do not know what my body is, nor my senses, nor my soul, or even that part of me which thinks what I am saying . . . Just as I do not know whence I came, so I do not know whither I am going. . . . Who would wish to have as a friend a man who argued this way? Who would choose him from among others as a confidant in his affairs? Who would resort to him in adversity? To what use in life could he possibly be turned?[5]

We are all waiting to die—not consciously—but we will do anything to avoid our body's ultimate decay. Some will be destroyed through fire in a matter of hours, while others, depending on climate and geography, will turn to mush; others, in desert areas, will just dry up. But we do everything to avoid these thoughts, things like believing in a god, working all the time, anything to avoid anticipating death.

I'm fifty-seven and I still bite my tongue and my lips. I make grimaces that have, through time, permanently damaged my jaws and tongue. I twist, knot, and pull my hair out; such a lovely life I've had. Many have had worse; many have had better. All I know is, mine has hurt very badly. It has been fun only about 5 percent of the time. Does that make life worth living?

---

5. Ibid., #427.

The Wendell Cocktail

I've mostly lived alone, but I was lucky to meet Mary, who showed me all kinds of woods—from the Olympics to the Everglades, from New Mexico to the Ontario waterways. Now I've seen all I needed to see; I've done all I wanted to do. I've tried hard to become a person I could be proud of, but there is just too much illness of the mind to give me any ease. Now mostly all I feel is disease and boredom, same-old, same-old.

My dog Maggie has been a great contributor to any happiness I've had. That is why she is in my will. I also realize that I am nothing and won't be remembered by anyone for long—not that it matters.

I'm afraid of death, yet I long for it. I've only wanted a reasonable amount of love. I learned from Mama to expect unconditional love. Yet I have alienated family members. I guess I speak my mind too much.

Low self-esteem is caused by a mind that has been battered by a parent, there is no assurance that what you think is, or could be, right. We are all liars to the extent that we say things that we may believe, but that really aren't true. We haven't looked at ourselves in an honest way, due to survival needs, maintaining status, or fear of confrontation. For many, self-examination is worse than having a root canal. Refusing to see something that is too painful to admit is common. High self-esteem is happiness, but it is accompanied by a tendency not to self-examine. Why look at something that works? So happiness depends on less openness since there is no need to ruminate or ponder anything, no need to go into painful areas of the self.

Peace: the most important spirit both within a person and in the world.

What have you done, people? You've locked him in a golden cage, made him bend toward your religion, and resurrected him from the grave. He is the god of nothing; you are the god of everything; he's inside you and me. So lean upon him gently and do not call upon him to save.

Wherever you're born and live, that's what religion you become. What does that tell you? It says to me that all religions have their merits and disadvantages, but it also says that the random element is at work; no one can choose where and from whom one was born.

5/15

My thoughts almost take over my sleeping hours; my dreams become indistinguishable from my waking thoughts. My dreams are terrible because they are beautiful, and I can't have them in real life: beautiful women from the 1920s being tender to me, giving me majestic ideas, giving me all that is wonderful in life.

2008

We live life day after day, month after month, year after year, and does it lead to something? Do we enjoy the journey?

We never keep to the present. We recall the past; we anticipate the future as if we found it too slow in coming and were trying to hurry it up, or we recall the past as if to stay its too rapid flight . . . we wander about in times that do not belong to us, and we do not think of the only one that does. . . . The fact is that the present usually hurts. . . . Thus we never actually live, but hope to live.[6]

Life feels like a dream. If dreams can seem so real, as real as the waking state, it doesn't seem too far-fetched to wonder what is really real.
    Within our little group of friends we must conform or we can't participate in that group anymore. I had an experience with a Christian group in 1973. I was slowly marginalized and then excluded because my questions were too annoying and unanswerable for them. Spiritual bigotry is as horrible as racial bigotry.
    Margi is this optimist that thinks of the best and beautiful in people, but that is because she has money. It is always those with money who have a more decidedly optimistic view. But with all their studies they have not learned that nothing has changed, that men are basically the same; competition will always rule the world. But do you honestly think that women would make a better world? Women have their own foibles.

5/22

I'm thinking that if there is a god he/she/it may not be a completely merciful and intelligent being. It takes a long time to make real change, and our lives are too short. We think in terms of our own lifetime; we're not able to think in terms of thousands of years. We need to learn other ways of thinking. Try to think of all the good and all the horrors that have actually taken place in your lifetime; then go back 100, 200, 300 years, and on and on. Then we may have a better sense of the human predicament.

We run headlong into the abyss after putting something in front of us to stop us seeing it.[7]

---

6. Pascal, *Pensées*, #47.
7. Ibid., #166.

The Wendell Cocktail

If I had a billion bucks I would buy an island, probably in the Fiji Islands. I'd buy a 1000-square-foot home, have a huge garden that I could eat from year round; windmills and solar panels. I would try for independence with a small boat, maybe a twenty-eight-foot sailboat. That's all I'd need, plenty of time to read, write, and think, to snorkel and dive.

Let me be with a kind and gentle person with soft skin and a peacefulness about them that will calm me, a soul that has a delicacy that renders me restful yet open, like the sound of the ocean and sand far away from humanity. A drizzle slowly putting me to sleep forever. Songwriters do that to me; Pink Floyd in some spots, the Moody Blues, Mozart. I am very tired and need relief, sleep, soft asylum. I could always handle the screwdriver feeling in my back better than I could the same going into my brain. I need to keep my head and mouth quiet, quiet.

The moments that make up a dull day: frittering away and wasting the hours, digging around on a piece of ground, waiting for someone or something to show you the way, tired and lying in the sunshine, staying in to watch the rain. I was young, and life is long, and there is time to kill today. Then suddenly it is ten years later. No one told me when to run, I missed the starting gun, and I run and try to catch up with the sunshine, but it's racing around to come up behind me again. I'm older, short of breath, and a day closer to death.[8]

Man finds nothing so intolerable as to be in a state of complete rest, without passions, without occupation, without diversion, without effort. Then he faces his nullity, loneliness, inadequacy, dependence, helplessness, emptiness. And at once there wells up from the depths of his soul boredom, gloom, depression, chagrin, resentment, despair.[9]

Don't show weakness: the code of all animals, including humans. Just internalize it, where it will eat away at you, munching away at your being.

What would we do with peace without conflict? Well, we would have to make a conflict; it's in our genes, in our very nature. We cannot just be satisfied with peace and love. It is in the nature of man to ruin it all. Who is to blame for this? Adam and Eve? I say bullshit.

---

8. This paragraph is a slightly modified version of the lyrics of Pink Floyd's "Dark Side of the Moon."

9. Pascal, *Pensées*, #622.

What does man today have to do with our forefathers—nothing. Either we go forward or we keep blaming all the generations that came before us. Maybe at one time there was love and care, but you can't tell me now that there is a master plan.

I would like to have had a dad who took me fishing and did things with me. Well, I didn't have that dad, so I went out of my way to be a good employer. And I was: employees like Mark and Doug, even after they went on to different work, treated me like a brother. I didn't do everything right, but by and large, I treated them well. I learned from my dad's treatment of me—and did the opposite. Maybe I would have been a good father, but I never wanted to pass my genes on to a child.

I found the strength to do a lot of backpacking; some trips were eighty miles long; most were from five to twenty miles. But the anger in me which I tried to hide would surface; it always had a strong hold on me, just waiting to surface. The one person, Mary, who had the most in common with me and who did the most hiking with me, eventually saw that anger. We were always just friends—kind of strange, all those nights far away and we never had sex.

7/25

I have a heart "flutter." A diagnostic test showed that the part of my heart that puts blood back into the system doesn't work as it should, but it's fine with me. I won't have any more operations. I have nothing to live for, no children, no one who can't live without me. I just wish it could be quick. I'm tired of suffering, and I don't like where humanity is going. I wish I could be with my mama, but I doubt that this will be the case.

When my Maggie goes, I'll say, it's okay, I've seen everything I want to see, hiking into the mountains, sitting on the beach when the moon is rising above the ocean. What more could one ask for? Sun lighting the moon as it comes up in the east. Nothing can be better than that. I'm also grateful for all the women with whom I've had a relationship. Waking up becomes harder each day; getting up is a major task. At my age it's okay to die. I do not know how I have lived so long, but it is enough to justify killing myself. What if one was in torture from cancer and no one ever came by to show their love? Well, it is the same.

When I die I think I know what I will see in my mind. I will see myself, seventeen years old, standing at the edge of the dock in Juanita Beach, Kirkland, Washington, depressed, as I had been since I was ten or eleven years old. I looked at the water I loved and still felt depressed, not teenage angst but mental illness, clinical depression.

The Wendell Cocktail

I am still depressed when I am surrounded by natural beauty; I am unable to enjoy the only thing, besides animals, that I love. You can't love or have passionate feelings when you are depressed, a state I've been in all my life, even when I was in love with a woman.

Now I'm just waiting to die. I hope to get a terminal disease so I won't be branded as a suicide, though I know I would probably have to suicide anyway for fear of the horrifying pain toward the end.

I enjoy being around people with different points of view. I not only find it interesting, but educational. [Those who do not care to be around] people with perspectives different than their own need to be flattered with information they already know because it takes a tremendous amount of cheerleading to keep their views (beliefs) strong. I'm the opposite. I love to hear others' thoughts, I want to know why they think as they do. You can easily understand why they think as they do just by listening rather than talking.

The soon-to-be-dead say that they are looking eternity in the face. The living use terms like "rest in peace." Rest and peace are concepts of the living. Death is nothingness, no rest, no peace, just nothing. Before one is born there is nothingness; I believe the same is true in death.

I am ashamed to say that a part of me was relieved when my father died. But I also hurt for a man who resented me all my life and could never bring himself to say, "I love you, Wendell." For a man, a pastor, to have so many people outside the family with strong emotional ties with him and then to have hardly any affection for his only son: it is extremely saddening and has caused me throughout my life to hate authority. Either I put men on pedestals or I hate them. Even when he wrote to me he could only say "affectionately, Dad." Maybe he felt he couldn't lie; I have no idea. Since I was little he had abused me; occasionally he would kick me or smack my ears. His main threat: "I'll cuff your ears!" I write these things only to try to show my—a little boy's—standpoint. I can count on one hand, with not many fingers, the kind things he did, and I wonder if these were done because of a threat from my mama.

Until you're forty or fifty you can't begin to understand those older than you. Youth looks upon the aged as almost alien, never realizing that they were once young and beautiful. It takes time and the pains involved in older age to see that the only difference is in perspective.

To go through life calm, cool, and collected seems unnatural. Violence has been the norm, not the exception; it is as much a part of man as of the world. But we live in a tunnel-vision time capsule, unable to see the large picture.

I used to be very frightened by the thought of nothingness. When I was eight years old I used to wake up in a cold sweat, thinking, what if there was nothing, not space, not planets, not stars. Why would a kid of average intelligence think these things? At fifteen I began reading philosophy, Sartre, Russell, Nietzsche, etc. Then I read Jung, Freud, and others. I've always wanted answers other than the ones given to me by my father and mother. In times of mental crisis I sometimes consulted Christians until at the age of forty-three I realized that the answers would have to come from me.

I love the oceans, fires, trees, birds—especially owls, crows, and ravens. I love the silence surrounding woods, rivers, lakes and ponds, flowers, the sky, the stars, the planets, the Milky Way, and all the black holes that cannot yet be seen. I love gravity, snow, mountains, valleys, clouds, the sun, and everything that can generate energy from natural sources, wind, sun, water. So much can be energized by such small means; a mere stream can cause enough power to energize several homes. In some geographical locations, sun can do it all. If we used all these sources, we would be free of the corporations that govern our lives and charge huge prices for simple utilitarian goods.

thirteen

2009

IN SPITE OF WENDELL'S fundamental disagreements with his parents' beliefs, I notice two beliefs they held in common. First, Wendell assumes that there is a "real you" to be discovered underneath all the layers of social "gracious"; second, he assumes that the "real you" will be rude, abrasive, unhappy, and full of hate. Although he has sometimes insisted that if he had not suffered from mental illness he would/could have been gentle, kind, and loving, his journals demonstrate that increasingly he came to think that the "real you" was antisocial, a "sinner" in the language of his parents' Calvinism.

> [Wendell's exact words:] *I man goes into a bank. I want to open a fucking bank account—lady says, what did you say?—he says, yo, I want to open a fucking bank account. She says, watch your language, and storms off. Bank manager comes over, what's the problem? Want to open a fucking bank account for $500 and man says to the teller, is this filth giving you a hard time?*
>
> *Social gracious [sic] are often just a way to put a mask on to hide the real you. It goes on constantly—I'm fine, how are you? We don't want to hear the truth, but we ask as a way of trying to be "friendly." I'm talking about the stuff that interferes with emotional honesty and deeply affects the personality.*
>
> *Horror and joy are constantly at war. Some times are low; some times are high; seldom is a happy medium struck. People with manic depression, now called bi-polar, are not reacting to circumstances, but instead are reacting to chemicals in their own brain. They are imprisoned by their own chemistry.*

3/31

I just want to go away to an asylum where my mind and body don't hurt anymore. Is that too much to ask? I'll even settle for the nothingness I came from. The asylum is a place where no one kills and people and animals live together in harmony, where all beings live off the vegetation and everyone shares. Communism, both as a political and a religious theory, was popular among those who wanted to live like this.

Mental illness always relates to the culture in which it exists. There are Amazon peoples who believe that they were born from dolphins. Tell that to a psychiatrist in North America and he will say that you are psychotic.

I believe that I will have an aneurism sometime in the next five years—fatal, I hope.

Possibly humans are the product of peaceful vegetarians combined with a more aggressive species. Maybe this is why we have both of these dimensions. We try to dominate other human beings, make them our slaves. But we also have an extremely emotional, empathizing, compassionate side. We have a tug of war between the two sides. This polarity of being has been the cause of much suffering.

Man is neither angel nor beast, and it is unfortunately the case that anyone trying to act the angel acts the beast.[1]

I heard a doctor on television say that marijuana can ease nausea and increase appetite. Other drugs for chemotherapy patients cost approximately $700 a month, but weed does it all at a fraction of the cost. He went on to say, "Euphoria as a side effect can't be too bad." It seems that we can feel good with impunity only on our last legs. If you can't find peace, you can search for another way, perhaps something illegal (marijuana) that can bring satisfaction: Plan B.

Micro levels of change is all beings can handle. We are almost genetically preset to be unable to take change any other way. Our bodies change slowly. If a fifteen-year-old were to wake up seventy it would be completely devastating. We gradually accustom ourselves to changes in our bodies and accept aging.

---

1. Pascal, *Pensées*, #678.

The Wendell Cocktail

7/14

The one who wears dark glasses sees the dark side of existence. Someone else does not wear the shades and sees the glass half full. Both see accurately. Since I was eleven or twelve I have had to fight against the dark side. I've been mired in it. Who knows what combination of environment and bio-chemicals created me. It's who I am. I don't think that I would even want to change. Therapy and drugs tried to change what couldn't be changed. Only a small percentage of addicts can stop using, because they can only feel and function "normally" when they are medicated to the point at which life feels all right.

I'd like to see my father again, for I know he had a good heart, mostly for others outside the home.

I was born to die; I don't know why I've lived so long.

I love my mother so much, but I also understand that she used me as a way to deny love and sex to Dad. I have no way of knowing what went on between them. All I have ever done was to try to understand and I know it's almost never that one side is right. Perhaps I got all the pampering from Mother because I got nothing but hatred and resentment from Dad. But there is much more to the story. All I know is what I went through. This is what has caused me to have a lifelong search for understanding everything. It has so traumatized me that I have not been able to live normally, but instead I torture and abuse myself. When one parent tells you you're no good, and the other that you can do no wrong, this is enough to cause anyone at age eleven to melt down as I did. I am fifty-eight years old; how much longer can I go on? I never thought I'd make it past twenty-five with the torture in my mind. Maybe it was Mom who gave me the strong side, the side that allowed me to fight for my freedom, and eventually my ability to make enough money to survive financially.

I heard only one argument between my parents. They were whispering, mad at each other about me. They thought they were protecting me from the absence of love between them. But a child has an almost animal intuition (sensitivity) toward what's really going on. The child knows, and it disturbs him greatly. My sisters saw different family dynamics while they were in the home. My parents' relationship deteriorated. Later, in their old age, they seemed to reconcile. I remember asking Mama about their relationship and she said, "Yes, now that we're older, things have become better"—weird, huh?

My life is quite lonely, but at the same time I don't really want anything else.

7/26

My parents were both good people because they were both trying to do right. Can we expect more of ourselves than in our own way to try to do our best?

My thoughts aren't original. I'm plagiarizing millions of people like myself from now and times past. We want to avoid the most painful reflections, but they are part of who we are. And the pain is worth it, if one is like me!

I've been involved with people who, through their words and actions, are "troubled." Yet I see positive sides to these people, so I continue to be with them in order to understand them more, and therefore, in a way, to understand myself.

> That's what I like
> a lonely road
> Where the treevine twines
> and the wrens sing
> a slow river below
> where on a hot day it's
> cool to the skin and no one but the
> other creatures are around

Few ever think about the enormity of this existence. We may be puppets. We have a gift to realize beauty; we also have a gift to realize horror. Did something up there in the cosmos do an experiment? So much of our makeup is to live in the now and not think beyond the now. I, like everyone, think of god as love, but what if it's not? If we are a mirror of it, then it can also make bad ideas.

Is it not as clear as day that man's condition is dual? If man had never been corrupted he would, in his innocence, confidently enjoy both truth and happiness, and if man had never been anything but corrupt, he would have no idea either of truth or bliss. . . . We perceive an image of the truth and possess nothing but falsehood, being equally incapable of absolute ignorance and certain knowledge.[2]

Moonlight drives to the sea where the water turns my mind into a vast array of thoughts; only good can come of sitting peacefully on the sand. Mesmerizing. Thoughts of life and death abound. Everyone is equal. We must all live and die. No one gets out of here alive.

---

2. Ibid., #131.

The Wendell Cocktail

When dreams die, people die. When there is no hope, people die. That's why I want to come back as a chickadee. Whether they realize it or not they are constantly living, surviving, working hard to perpetuate their species. We are all hardwired for this.

I feel like going back to age twelve when I was in Ryther. I was somewhere between psychotic and emotionally depressed, but back then there was little distinction. My parents put me in Ryther as a last resort. I was in such pain; I could never describe it. Pain is supposed to make you stronger, but unlike cancer mental pain seems to come from nothing, from hell. It makes you a drooling idiot. The only difference between then and now is that I will not put my life in the hands of therapists and psychiatrists who know less than I do. As one of them told me, after thirty years of talking and chemical "cures," Wendell knows and is very wise.

Being depressed is feeling fear all the time. The physical effects are cotton mouth, tingling going from your heart to your legs, hyper-alertness at times, catatonic at others, strong awareness of death; it never leaves your head. I feel like a wounded animal that seeks a hiding place so it can die with dignity, peace.

Patients have a right to refuse treatment. Doctors cannot touch you if you tell them, no thank you, I don't want your help. I want no force outside myself to tell me what I have to do. I need to control my body and mind; legally I have this right.

People who want hard drugs or soft drugs will find them. If drugs were legal all the violence surrounding drugs would stop and those who use would take responsibility—or not. I don't believe society would become a free-for-all state of drug-induced horror—no more than it already is. The government should not be able to tell you what you may ingest.

You are wondering why it is taking me so long to die. Well. I have been a courageous fighter against my depression—something you will never begin to appreciate. I've gone through so much suffering you've never heard about. You have no idea—none. One has to walk in another's shoes to have empathy; very few even have sympathy, because people still believe that mental illness is a form of laziness, or it's something like the feelings they get from grief. It has nothing to do with the so-called "blues"; it is a condition not only of the mind, but also of the body. I feel strange sensations like paranoia and fear for no other reason than that my chemicals are not doing the right thing. I think that to recover I would have to have a lobotomy or shock treatment. I've tried most of the drugs and they've had little effect. Unconsciousness seems to be the only relief. I started with Mellaril, an anti-psychotic, when I was twelve; that drug alone could alter the brain. I think that it was the only tranquilizer available in 1964. It made me catatonic. Sure, I slept well but, like Seconal, it had huge side effects.

I went to my dream beach all alone thinking this would hearten me, only to realize that I was just another stone on the beach. No peace, no relaxation, just loneliness and depression. In time, because of people walking on me, the stone that I am will disintegrate into sand.

How can we trust our minds? We are almost robots; we don't have the ability to look at ourselves objectively; we have tunnel vision, even when we think we know. We are babes in the woods. We think we're so smart. We're destroying the planet—how smart is that? Are we asleep? Yes, and I think that we will be until we truly evolve.

All our reasoning comes down to surrendering to feeling.... Reason is available but can be bent in any direction. And so there is no rule.[3]

10/20

> I have been in the dark woods, but
> I have found some food and
> I've made my way from those woods
> to the edge of the forest.
> I can see the bright fields and the glimmering
> sea beyond.
> Hope I can get there.

When I die I want any money I have to help the really downtrodden: children, people with mental illness, addiction services for the poor. I think it's a crime that poor people can't get the help they need when they want to get off the addiction cycle. Mark crawled into a treatment center having "hit bottom" and was turned away. This is wrong.

I need soft asylum, sanctuary, a place to hide. I cannot work my mind anymore; it only comes up with horrifying scenarios.

A brief glimpse at all of this: unborn, born, then dead again, nothingness. I began thinking about this when I was seven or eight. So far I have only come to terms with the reality that dead is the same as non-existent.

---

3. Ibid., # 530.

The Wendell Cocktail

"Seek and you will find" is the biggest crock I've ever known. I say this with some anger but also with great sadness and melancholy. I was told that [seeking] would do the trick. What more can I do. I've prayed and prayed to the "Almighty," but my brain does not compute. I am a person who cannot see things that others seem to grasp.

Psychiatrists and psychologists are in the controlling mode, level 5. They are like Dad, uncomfortable with anyone who has any control at all left to their poor shattered being. If you ask questions that are important to you, they begin to withdraw, physically and emotionally. Before I was twenty-five or twenty-six the counselors I spent time with carried themselves in a professional manner, no subject was taboo as in later experiences.

I did get my money's worth in 1994 when I was forty-three years old. My psychiatrist gave me a new diagnosis; that was, that I was OCD (obsessive-compulsive disorder) first, and depression second. This made perfect sense to me. The itches, the biting of lips, the compulsive swallowing—I couldn't stop swallowing night and day. That was the cause of a very great depression at about age twenty. I could not understand what was taking place. Judi left me because of my OCD and depression. She and her parents saw things in me that I had been repressing since I was ten. Now that I've lived so long, I think it is only some inner strength, my genes, that have moved me—I can't say forward, but on. I still can't love the kid I was; I have internalized my dad's hatred for me.

I'm happy that I have not passed on my genes; they will die with me. But mental illness is alive and well in our family. I see very troubling things about my nephews, perhaps not to the extent of my own mental illness but nonetheless some similar symptoms.

I think that it is very understandable that I have been self-absorbed to the extent I have, and why it has extended beyond me to bigger things. Even monks have a support system that enables them to confront themselves and not long to die because of the pain. Confrontation has its merits, but escape allows one to survive. Even denial, as long as it works, helps.

People deal with things in such different ways; this amazes me. How can I find peace? I've done everything I know how to do and it won't come. I am lucky that I have had my own experiences of woods and women; these were very important to me. Sex and the woods are so important; one takes you to the brink of death and the other makes you see yourself in real terms as an animal among trees that will outlive you by many moons.

I need release; life should not be as horrifying as it has been for me. The mental illness has been far beyond anything that can be described. Maybe all my seeking is just an escape from the other pain; it is so overwhelming that I hope the end is near.

The more I explore, the fewer answers I have. Perhaps it takes a bit more to want to end your life, but not much. You have to already have a depression background, dysthymia or whatever. If the ticks, the biting and bleeding of my gums were the only thing, it might be different.

When one is told that they are loved, it calms you down, makes you feel secure, and also gives you an affinity with others, makes you want to help others, do the right thing. But when children—or anyone—are bombarded with criticism, it can only be a road to ruin.

Where the conflict is between love and hate—and I don't use the word "hate" lightly—I truly believe that my father's actions showed a consistent pathological basis, that he resented me, as I've already discussed. But that is too much for the mind of an eight- to twelve-year-old; a breakdown is inevitable when one [parent] hates you, and one loves you.

I feel great compassion towards suffering beings, human or animal. I think I inherited this from Mother, but perhaps it is also the result of the horrors I experienced as a child. Both play major roles. I also have an appreciative eye toward what I find beautiful, realizing that beauty serves nature. A flower is made primarily for the insect that will serve the perpetuation of its species, and vice versa. One cannot live without the other.

I believe that actions, not thoughts, are important. Only fascists judge a person by his thoughts. Many evaluate people not on the basis of their kindness, thoughtfulness, or generosity, but based on their lifestyle. This is wrong. What is important is self-knowledge and knowledge of the world. To try your best to be decent and generous, and when you fail, to ask forgiveness, is all that should be important. Whether one drinks or smokes, whether one has an appearance that is not considered "trustworthy," whether one likes to watch certain programs on television, whether one likes to race motorbikes, enjoys the noise of fast cars, or enjoys hotels or motels rather than "roughing it," has nothing to do with whether the person is kind and generous. But Homo sapiens have not learned to put the important in the forefront and the unimportant to the side.

We all have potential for violence. My father was about to strike me when I had my neck brace on in 1974. After that, I began to see things slightly differently, not that I hadn't realized his potential for anger and violence. I saw him a few times when I was seven or eight throw yard tools into the garage and I was frightened. After he kicked me twice when I was seven as I sat on the floor by my bed,

I realized that violent behavior could happen again, as it did. Most important, I realize that I inherited some of my own anger problems from him.

To change neurotic misery into common unhappiness: the goal of the Freudian talking cure. But it is dangerous to put your mind into the hands of therapists. It may be of great aid, but it's as likely that one will be harmed as that one will be helped.

When I was twenty-one I was taken to Western Washington State Mental Asylum on the recommendation of a psychiatrist. I was very bothered by cracks in the cement—couldn't walk on them without feeling a psychic shock. Severe depression with psychotic tendencies was the diagnosis. I was "emotionally disturbed." And yet perhaps because of this misery I have some wisdom. I just constantly have to check myself or I feel I'll fall off a cliff; it's not a very joyous way to live.

Why do I write? Because it's the only way I can feel that there is some significance in my life—[my journals are] my babies. I realize, however, that simply recording my thoughts and experiences means nothing.

I am a humble seeker of truth. To understand would mean more to me than all the money in the world. Since this will never happen, however, I'll take the money.

I need to go to a beautiful place with complete silence and pay in blood, sweat, and tears for my addictive excesses.

Understanding an idea honestly and without prejudice should be a personal goal. Why don't we have the guts to do this in our everyday experience? For me, this informs the "Wendell Miles" experience!

Ways to escape oneself: drugs, rationalization, intellectualizing (which was my way for many years), and religion. Also addictions, whether sex, eating or drinking; even work can be an escape. Until one can embrace one's own darkness and light, little can be learned about oneself. And we all have both.

If one is not feeling well, reality is distorted. You become a bitter person when you don't feel well for thirty to forty years.

People with whom we have no relationship—strangers—can't be judged. We do not know how much weight another person is carrying. If we could keep our judgments only toward those we know, the world would be a better place. But most of us continually judge those of whom we have no understanding.

Why, if there is a god, are things so hard? These thoughts torture me. I get so confused, I just want to be unconscious—to have some relief from all the suffering. And according to people like Dad, suffering is all your own fault; you must have done something to deserve it. If there is a god, then life should be easier. Why can't we all be in a state of euphoria? The myth of Adam and Eve tries to explain why humans deserve all the guilt.

Why can't I have a normal mind like "most"?

Is it any wonder that some people say "to here, and no further"—my life must end, for in all my diligent, hard-working ways, nothing has helped—not God, Jesus, or any other of the religious leaders. Mankind is probably too scared to face facts; to see our history in scientific ways makes faith difficult. Reading this, people will say, how sad, he didn't understand.

It is my destiny to not know. I only want one thing: to see my dear mother again. Why can't I be like others and strongly believe that I will? I don't know why, other than genetics and environment. I started being sick in the head at a very early age; I don't know anything else. I want peace above anything else; this was why I moved to Colville, but wherever you go, you are still there. It's not like I'm running from something I shouldn't have done, although the pain of my past haunts me. I spent most of my twenties and thirties running toward things and I have some wonderful memories, especially of backpacking in the woods, seeing things that most people never see. But ultimately I didn't find what I needed there. I hiked five miles alone to Boulder Lake twice, but I was afraid when I was alone; I could never get beyond it. Maybe now I could if my body would hold up.

I can't stop crying; my heart beats fast, and I feel on the verge of panic. I have felt this way often throughout my life. When was it different?

Death, the ultimate disappearing act. You not only disappear from others, but from yourself. As you were before the seed hit the egg—that's death. Not to worry; did you worry before you had consciousness? Death is as normal as eating a meal.

Death: the disappearance of consciousness, plain and simple. Try to enjoy life, eat, drink, and try to enjoy the moment, for we have nothing else. It's just that these very attempts are so much more complex. We must enjoy before the good times turn to bad; it's a tightrope act. I'm on a tightrope; one side's hate and one is hope, but the altitude really gets to me.

I have wanted to be unconscious since I was eleven, not necessarily dead, but gone. This is not right or normal. I have no other way to perceive or judge myself except by my own experience. I have nothing to trust but my senses.

The Wendell Cocktail

Man's greatness comes from knowing he is wretched; a tree does not know it is wretched.[4]

I need a place to hide; can you find me sanctuary, a soft asylum? I can't take it anymore. I can't find that place with anything other than chemicals. In the past, even in the grip of mental illness, I've always had the ability to find asylum within my mind, but no more.

I'm just so tired.

---

4. Pascal, *Pensées*, #114.

PART 3

Margaret's Journal

fourteen

THE LAST FEW DAYS

3/20/2010

Wendell is seriously ill. He has internal bleeding, a heart aneurysm, tumors in his lungs, gastrointestinal blockage—just a mess. His blood pressure is 89/45. He is obviously in terrible shape, but his doctor does not treat him, always wanting more tests. Today Rita, his longtime companion, called to tell me how serious his illness is. He has lost thirty or thirty-five pounds, and he only weighed 165 to begin with; he declines from day to day. Since she is not a relative, his doctor will not return her calls, so she asked me to call his office to ask for an immediate appointment. She does not have medical power of attorney because the form was not completed. It requires the signatures of two witnesses and he would not let Rita bring people to the house. After I called, he got an appointment the next day.

    I am learning to distinguish anxiety from grief. Anxiety is primarily about me: What should I be doing? What can I do? Surely I should be doing something. I should be fixing this, or at least expressing my love for Wendell more effectively. Grief is about Wendell. I see again the sweet little boy in a beige overcoat, looking a bit anxious. I see the adult Wendell at Mother's funeral, handsome in his camel overcoat. I grieve that little boy, that man, who has had such a harsh life, who has seen the beauty and has been wounded, not saved by it.

3/31/10

Wendell is in the hospital. The heart specialist he finally saw said that he would have died in a few days if he hadn't gotten treatment. Rita saved his life by insisting that he go to the heart specialist and then to the hospital.

The Wendell Cocktail

Now he is going crazy in the hospital, impatient to get home. He told me on the telephone that he was awakened at 3:30 a.m. the night before to be weighed. He complained "courteously," as he said, so a plaque was placed above his bed that read "Cluster care." He said it has done no good. I wanted to say, "Yeah, but you could be dead by now." I have to hope that he doesn't resent Rita for saving his life! Wendell is very frustrating to deal with.

Wendell checked himself out of the hospital Friday, signing a form that he understood that he was doing this "against medical advice." He had a heart attack (or stroke) in the hospital, not major, but with some damage to his heart. So now he's home alone again, waiting for the next heart attack. I have used up my present allotment of anxiety on him so now I feel numb, asking, like Mother, "What next?"

4/7/10

Next was that Wendell had a massive stroke and was flown from Colville by helicopter to Holy Family Hospital in Spokane. Rita called to tell me this at 11:30 last night. Then a doctor called at 1:30 a.m. to figure out with me what to do with Wendell. I told her that Wendell was very clear that he did not want surgery. She said that we won't know for several days how impaired Wendell is by the stroke. I didn't sleep for the rest of the night.

This morning I called to confer with Dorothy on whether she agreed that we need to honor Wendell's wishes concerning treatment and, after talking with Dennis, she agreed that we do. So that means, I think, that he will die quite soon. This morning Rita called to say that he also has pneumonia now. He is unconscious, in an induced coma.

4/25/10

Wendell died on April 22 at 12:45 a.m. I was with him in the hospital for several days, talking with doctors and, with Rita, making the decision to take him off life supports (ventilator, feeding tube, etc.). An excruciating decision, but one that was quite clear. Wendell had told everyone that if he had "something bad" he would not accept surgery and did not want to be in a nursing facility for the rest of his life. The neurologist showed us X-rays of the several strokes he had, and was continuing to have. Both sides of his brain had blood clots and swelling that would eventually be reabsorbed, but it made no sense to keep him alive since he refused to have the necessary valve replacement surgery. The doctor explained the best-case scenario: if he had valve replacement surgery, and if he worked very hard for about a year, he might regain 30 percent of his mental and physical capacity. But he would be in a nursing home for the rest of his life.

For two days he breathed with difficulty, completely unresponsive, eyes open but seeing nothing. An hour or two before he died the neurologist who had explained his condition to us came to see me. He was very kind, telling me (not in so many words, but by describing how terribly damaged Wendell's body was) that I had made the right decision about removing him from life supports.

I was planning to stay overnight with him, but about 12:30 a.m. his breathing became very light and soon there were six to ten seconds between breaths. Then they stopped. Although I hadn't called her, a nurse came into the room. I told her that I thought he had stopped breathing and she began to massage his chest strongly and call him, "Wendell! Wendell!" I said, "Oh, please don't pull him back." For what?

Wendell let himself die. He signed himself out of the hospital "against medical advice." And he declined surgery to replace a damaged heart valve. If not precisely suicide, this was at least suicidal behavior. But I prefer to think of it simply as a life choice, to be respected as we respected his often-stated wishes in removing him from life supports.

The morning after I got home from Wendell's death, I got up, raised the blinds, and there, on the roof slightly lower than my bedroom window, was a dead songbird. Rita had just reminded me the morning before that Wendell loved birds. I asked Owen to remove the bird, but he forgot. It lay there for two days and then was gone. I imagine—why not?—that Wendell sent me a message through the intricate connectedness of the universe. A friend told me that Buddhists believe that the spirit lingers around the deceased's loved ones for forty-nine days after death. I might have preferred a live bird but, come to think of it, I was probably visited by many live birds and just didn't notice. But a dead bird got my attention!

Today, one week later, while I was eating lunch, a huge wild turkey strode calmly across the deck, flew to the fence, and disappeared. Wild turkeys had not been seen in the Berkeley hills for several years. Another bird from Wendell? This one was big enough to get my attention, and this time, it was alive!

For awhile I rehearsed compulsively in my mind the "more" I could have done for Wendell. Since this was utterly fruitless, I reminded myself instead of the things I did with and for Wendell that I'm happy about. I'm happy that I was with him when he died, holding his hand, stroking his face, freshening the cold washcloth on his forehead, and telling him I love him, that he can let go, that Mother is waiting for him. I had not, by then, read his journal and did not know that this was his dearest—really his only—wish. I focused on surrounding him with love, telling him that he is perfectly safe in the universe. I also repeated Granny Brown's words of sympathy, "Poor little body."

EPILOGUE

WENDELL IS BEYOND HELP or comfort. I am left with the quandary about how best to help my son, Ric, who suffers from similarly debilitating depression. For approximately thirty years of his adult life, I gave him the equivalent of a social security income, hoping to provide a platform from which he could launch himself in some kind—any kind—of life and work. This didn't happen, so I was simply an "enabler," and told so repeatedly by well-meaning friends. Two years ago he initiated a petition for a Supplemental Security Income, which he now receives and more or less lives on. In the second half of each month, he is broke and bicycles daily ten miles (each way) to the nearest soup kitchen. Nothing has helped him—neither three month-long detoxification and rehabilitation programs, nor psychotherapy, nor Alcoholics Anonymous.

Nineteen years ago, in 1992, Ric wrote to me:

> *Dear Mom,*
> *Well? Here's a short update on what's going on with me these days. Believe me, it's not easy for me to write to you or anybody. I've never been so angry and depressed at the world as I've been now for awhile. I'm still in the same place [a group halfway house]. And there ain't no way to describe this place in a way that would give you an idea of how I'm feeling. Out of twenty-eight residents there isn't a single one that I have similar interests with other than substance abuse. And despite having this in common, there isn't a one that I would ever get high with. I have felt alone most of my life, but never have I felt so bitterly and confusingly alone as this.*
> *Yes! I'm an alcoholic/addict. It's also very obvious to me that I developed this disease through extreme depression that goes way, way, way back. Before I ever smoked my first pot or drank my first beer. Weed and alcohol are still the only thing that allows me to escape momentarily, and give me a short period of peace of mind.*

The Wendell Cocktail

> *Being sober for three weeks has allowed me none! The experts' response? "It's because you're coming off the drugs, Ric. Give it time."*
>
> *I'm not rationalizing using again. I really don't give a damn about what people think. And I don't have to rationalize to myself either. I know I'll turn back to it if that's my only release. I don't plan on living with this pain for the remainder of my life, nonstop! I think I know how Marilyn and Wendell have felt or do feel. I'll try any new idea, like a drug, whatever. Counseling and AA are not going to solve my unhappiness. They could solve other living issues (AA at least) I know.*
>
> *But haven't I tried these things enough to know that something else is going on? I can't pinpoint depression. I just remember always having been depressed and insecure. Do I feel that where I'm physically at now is going to make me feel better? There is no such thing as magic. This is no threat in order to get help out of here. I'm here because it's here or the streets. And perhaps I can somehow (how?) drag myself into a slightly better situation? I don't know. I know motivation to live ain't getting no better. The experts tell me, "Give yourself some time." Doesn't anybody know? It goes toooo far back! If you think I had a happy childhood, you are not only way off, but in a strong form of denial yourself. It's not your fault. It's not Dad's fault. I don't even think it's my fault, really! Knowing whose fault it is wouldn't help me in the slightest anyway.*
>
> *Well, I'm going to close here. I'm tired of writing and only feeling stuck anyway. Let me wish you a happy Mother's Day and birthday, as I probably won't get around to writing again beforehand. I really just want to keep a distance from everyone here for awhile anyway. I'm done here with all my friends and family for awhile. I need to do this. I am too bitter at people. And I don't want to act like I'm not. I do love you, Mom.*
>
> *Ric*

Today Ric lives alone; for him that's an improvement over the group living he complained of in 1992. Yet his letter describes with precision his present mental state. His body, however, is almost twenty years older, exhausted, and painful. As he wrote, the problem is not so much locating available resources as it is that he will not agree to the kinds of help on offer. He refuses to live with either his father or me. He refuses to live with people in any situation.

Twelve-step programs, with their insistence on "tough love," urge family members to withdraw all financial and emotional support from addicts. For a time I attended Al-Anon meetings hoping for advice and comfort. I heard many tales of what I considered cruelty to addicted family members. One woman boasted of locking her fifteen-year-old son out of her home in the Boston winter. Finally, for several months, I consulted a psychiatrist who specialized in treating family members of addicts. She told me, "Eighty percent of addicts from whom families withdraw all support are jarred into recovery; no one talks about the other twenty percent, and they are at extremely high risk for suicide." The "tough love" strategy has dominated, and continues to inform Americans' assumptions about how addiction should be treated. It has taken me many years to find an alternative. The following paragraphs describe the thinking process by which I have come to adopt an attitude and behavior toward my son characterized by compassion. Bear with me!

When I began to write this book, I assumed that mental illness—a problem of immense personal, communal, and social magnitude—is, or should be, curable. If sufficient resources were put into research, I thought, cures could be found. But what if this is not the case? What if the idea that mental suffering can be prevented or cured is illusory, the product of a worldview that "presupposes a world of objects that are susceptible to measurement, experiment, calculation, exposure, comprehension, and mastery?"[1] What if mental illness cannot be "mastered"?

Eric Krakauer traces Americans' confidence that there is no limit to what can be mastered to Descartes' identification of the thinking subject as the essential person—*cogito ergo sum*. He calls this identification "the founding gesture of the modern age."[2] In Descartes' description, the thinking subject positions thought or perception over against all objects. In medical science as in technology, the subject "presupposes that all that is can be known and mastered."[3] From this perspective, even death becomes an object to be managed; but instead of achieving this goal, the effort has only "prolonged and complicated dying and propagated suffering." Moreover, in the process of delaying death, emotional aspects of dying that until quite recently were all-important now appear insignificant.

> Deferring death becomes more important than attending to the soul or preparation for the afterlife [according to the dying person's beliefs] or the next life . . . becomes more important than

---

1. Krakauer, "To Be Freed from the Infirmity of (the) Age," 386.
2. Ibid., 385.
3. Ibid., 386.

being with or saying farewell to loved ones, reconciling with estranged loved ones, or being [in one's own] home.[4]

Krakauer proposes an alternative to the goal of mastery: palliative care. Palliative care responds to the patient's *suffering*, rather than attempting to prolong life. "What calls is suffering, and attention to suffering reveals that life-sustaining technology is not always called for . . . [Palliative care] *lets dying be*."[5] In other words, "palliative care does not approach dying exclusively with the goal of mastery."[6] Hospices, practicing palliative care, attend first and foremost to alleviation of the patient's suffering.

Hospice, in its contemporary form, was founded in the 1960s in Great Britain, but hospitals for the poor, the sick, and the dying have existed since antiquity.[7] Before medical science developed technologies for curing illness and/or prolonging life, all hospitals were, in effect, hospices. Palliative care addressed not only physical suffering, but also the full range of the patient's misery, including feelings of terrible loss—of life, of everything the person has built—terror of death, and within Christianity, fear of the Last Judgment so vividly pictured in virtually every church in Christendom. In the late medieval hospital at Colmar, patients were regularly brought to the chapel to contemplate Grunewald's Isenheim Altarpiece, which depicted the suffering Christ as bearing the same grotesque skin diseases as those of the patients. Reassured that Christ shared their suffering, patients prayed for either a cure or for the strength and courage to bear their own suffering.

Gabor Maté and others have extended the range of palliative care beyond care for the dying. Maté, a Canadian physician who works with addicts in the slums of Vancouver, British Columbia, describes his goal as harm reduction.

> The issue in medical practice is always how best to help the patient. If a cure is possible *and* probable without doing greater harm, then cure is the objective. When it isn't—and in most chronic medical conditions cure is not [the] expected outcome—the physician's role is to help the patient with the symptoms and to reduce the harm done by the disease process. . . . [H]arm reduction means

---

4. Ibid., 390.
5. Ibid., 391.
6. Ibid.

7. In contemporary hospices, the patient's doctor must state that, according to his educated guess, the patient has less than six months to live.

making the lives of afflicted human beings more bearable, more worth living.[8]

Maté's clinic provides support for addicts who choose abstinence, but for those who don't, he writes, "[W]e do not make our valuation of addicts as worthwhile human beings dependent on their making choices that please us." He quotes Dr. Bruce Perry: "We need to be very loving, very accepting, and very patient with people who have these problems. And if we are, they will have a much higher probability of getting better."[9]

Maté provides heroin users with methadone, which transfers their dependence to "a narcotic that is legal, that is safe if ingested properly, and that prevents them from having to prostitute themselves, steal, and beg to avoid withdrawal."[10] No such drug exists for cocaine users, and not all heroin users accept methadone as a substitute. Maté's compassion for the addicts with whom he works extends to the provision of "heroin or morphine unadulterated by who-knows-what impurities, to be self-injected in a clean environment with uncontaminated needles." He writes, "We are neither condoning nor encouraging addiction: the addiction exists and will continue to savage that person's life no matter what . . . Our only choice is between compassion and indifference."[11] Recognizing that physicians and caregivers do not have the ability to "save" addicts, Maté responds to their vulnerability with compassion—the only option that does not increase harm and perpetuate suffering. Maté practices palliative care in a different context than that of hospice.

Could a *realistic* and compassionate approach to the suffering of dual diagnosis (coexisting conditions) patients also be useful for the treatment of mental illness? *Both* addiction and mental illness have been understood as diseases, with the attendant assumption that we should seek mastery over them. *But neither addiction nor mental illness is a disease; both are conditions that must be lived with.*[12] If curing either condition is unlikely or impossible, why not alleviate the patient's *suffering*, making her life "more bearable, more worth living"?

---

8. To the objection that compassion to addicts "enables" drug and alcohol use, Maté responds, "There is no evidence from anywhere in the world that harm-reduction measures encourage drug use." *Hungry Ghosts*, 332, 335.

9. Ibid., 336.

10. Ibid.

11. Ibid., 338.

12. Ibid., 138.

The Wendell Cocktail

A compassionate approach to dual diagnosis patients is a hard sell in contemporary American society, although some physicians and (usually) small, nonprofit clinics do practice it. Governmental efforts to master mental illness and drug addictions consist primarily of the enormously expensive and ineffective "war on drugs." Yet the war on drugs has been dramatically unsuccessful. The daily use of marijuana among high school seniors more than doubled between the mid-1990s and the mid-2000s, and deaths from drug overdoses doubled between 1999 and 2005. Clearly, the war on drugs has not worked, yet the United States government opposes "decriminalization and harm-reduction programs anywhere on the globe."[13] An exaggerated fear of addiction even prevents the provision of adequate pain relief to countless individuals for mental and physical illness.[14]

Marc Miringoff, professor of social welfare policy, invented an index of the nation's social health that included sixteen indicators, among them infant mortality, child abuse, child poverty, teenage suicide, drug abuse, high school dropouts, adult unemployment, health insurance coverage, old-age poverty and health costs, homicides, food insecurity, affordable housing, and income inequality. Reporting annually since 1987 (with the latest completed report in 2008), the premise of the index is that no one indicator can give the full picture of America's social health, but the combination of these sixteen indicators can allow researchers to rate how America is doing. In 2008, the Index of Social Health stood at 55.5 (out of a possible 100). "Overall, between 1970 and 2008, the Index declined from 66.2 to 55.5" despite periods of economic growth.[15] In a 2008 interview, Marque-Luisa Miringoff, professor of sociology and director of the Institute for Innovation in Social Policy, reported that America has the highest child poverty rate in the industrialized world, and forty-five million Americans have no health insurance.

American society is becoming meaner by the day to vulnerable and marginal people, providing fewer and fewer safety nets. Many Americans are deeply hostile to the suggestion that compassionate palliative care is appropriate for addicts and the mentally ill, who are seen by many people as bringing their problems upon themselves. Yet there is substantial evidence

---

13. Ibid., 289.

14. For discussion of the costs and ineffectiveness of the war on drugs, see Maté, *Hungry Ghosts*, ch. 25. According to the World Health Organization, "nearly five million people a year with advanced cancer receive inadequate or no pain relief, along with another 1.4 million with late-stage AIDS" (288).

15. Miringoff, *Index of Social Health*.

that compassionate care can produce results beneficial both to addicts and to society. Lower crime rates, reduced rates of disease-promoting needle-sharing, increased participation in detoxification and rehabilitation programs, and fewer deaths from contaminated street drugs are among the documented and recognized benefits of palliative (or harm-reduction) programs. These programs do not "fight addiction" but act as entry points to the possibility of recovery by providing "a more bearable life, a life worth living."[16]

I have not found available and affordable compassionate palliative care for my son. But his father and I agree to practice such care insofar as we are able. Compassion will not change Ric's determination to treat himself with the only effective medicine he has found. His life is dramatically damaged and shortened by alcohol, but ultimately I respect his experience of *what helps*. When I visit him, I am amazed that a life that looks to me so bleak, largely reduced to riding his bicycle and listening to the radio, nevertheless allows him, on the whole, to remain cheerful and friendly, to love his family, and to maintain a sense of humor.

Ric, Wendell, my father and grandfather: I hold you, needy and beautiful, in my heart. As Plato said, "The beautiful things are difficult."[17]

16. Maté, *Hungry Ghosts*, 343.
17. Plato, *Greater Hippias* 304e, 339.

BIBLIOGRAPHY

Adler, Patricia A., and Peter Adler. *The Tender Cut: Inside the Hidden World of Self-Injury.* New York: New York University Press, 2011.
Angell, Marcia. "The Emperor's New Drugs: Exploding the Antidepressant Myth." *The New York Review of Books*, July 14, 2011, 20–22.
———. "The Epidemic of Mental Illness: Why?" *The New York Review of Books*, June 23, 2011, 20–22.
Bonaventure, Saint. *The Mind's Road to God.* Translated by George Boas. Indianapolis: Bobbs-Merrill, 1953.
Carlat, Daniel. *Unhinged: The Trouble with Psychiatry: A Doctor's Revelations about a Profession in Crisis.* New York: Free Press, 2010.
Corin, Ellen. "The 'Other' of Culture in Psychosis: The Ex-Centricity of the Subject in Psychosis." In *Subjectivity: Ethnographic Investigations*, edited by João Biehl, Byron Good, and Arthur Kleinman, 273–314. Berkeley: University of California Press, 2007.
Custance, John. *Wisdom, Madness, and Folly: The Philosophy of a Lunatic.* New York: Pellegrini & Cudahy, 1952.
Dostoyevsky, Fyodor. *The Idiot.* Translated by David McDuff. London: Penguin, 2004.
Dreyfus, Hubert L., and Paul Rabinow. *Michel Foucault: Beyond Structuralism and Hermeneutics.* Chicago: University of Chicago Press, 1982.
Fingarette, Herbert. *Heavy Drinking: The Myth of Alcoholism as a Disease.* Berkeley: University of California Press, 1988.
———. *Self-Deception.* 2nd ed. Berkeley: University of California Press, 2000.
Freud, Sigmund. *Civilization and Its Discontents.* Edited and translated by J. Strachey. In vol. 21 of the standard edition of *The Complete Psychological Works of Sigmund Freud.* London: Hogarth, 1962.
Foucault, Michel. *The Foucault Reader.* Edited by Paul Rabinow. New York: Pantheon, 1984.
Kierkegaard, Søren. *Kierkegaard's The Concept of Dread.* Translated by Walter Lowrie. Princeton: Princeton University Press, 1957.
Kleinman, Arthur, and Erin Fitz-Henry. "The Experiential Basis of Subjectivity: How Individuals Change in the Process of Societal Transformation." In *Subjectivity: Ethnographic Investigations*, edited by João Biehl, Byron Good, and Arthur Kleinman, 52–65. Berkeley: University of California Press, 2007.
Krakauer, Eric L. "To Be Freed from the Infirmity of (the) Age: Subjectivity, Life-Sustaining Treatment, and Palliative Medicine." In *Subjectivity: Ethnographic*

Bibliography

Investigations, edited by João Biehl, Byron Good, and Arthur Kleinman, 381–96. Berkeley: University of California Press, 2007.

Kristeva, Julia. *Black Sun: Depression and Melancholia*. Translated by Leon S. Roudiez. New York: Columbia University Press, 1989.

Maté, Gabor. *In the Realm of Hungry Ghosts: Close Encounters with Addiction*. Berkeley: North Atlantic Books, 2010.

Macy, Joanna, and Anita Barrows, editors and translators. *A Year with Rilke: Daily Readings from the Best of Rainer Maria Rilke*. New York: HarperCollins, 2009.

McNally, Richard S. *What Is Mental Illness?* Cambridge: Harvard University Press, 2011.

Miringoff, Marque-Luisa. *Index of Social Health*. In *America's Social Health*, 69–90. Armonk, NY: M. E. Sharpe, 2008.

Pascal, Blaise. *Pensées*. Translated by A. J. Krailsheimer. New York: Penguin, 1975.

Plato. *Greater Hippias*. Translated by David R. Sweet. In *The Roots of Political Philosophy: Ten Forgotten Socratic Dialogues*, edited by Thomas L. Pangle. Ithaca: Cornell University Press, 1987.

Rilke, Rainer Maria. *Duino Elegies*. Translated by J. B. Leishman and Stephen Spender. New York: Norton, 1939.

Sheets-Johnstone, Maxine. *The Corporeal Turn: An Interdisciplinary Reader*. Exeter, UK: Imprint Academic, 2009.

———. *The Roots of Morality*. University Park: University of Pennsylvania Press, 2008.

Styron, William. *Darkness Visible: A Memoir of Madness*. New York: Random House, 1990.

Whitaker, Robert. *Anatomy of an Epidemic: Magic Bullets, Psychiatric Drugs, and the Astonishing Rise of Mental Illness in America*. New York: Crown, 2010.

Wieseltier, Leon. "Saul Bellow's Quest for the Vernacular Sublime." *The New York Times Sunday Book Review*, November 21, 2010, 13.

www.ingramcontent.com/pod-product-compliance
Lightning Source LLC
Chambersburg PA
CBHW030050100426
42734CB00038B/990